ISBN 978-1-332-10959-3
PIBN 10285903

1 MONTH OF
FREE
READING

at

www.ForgottenBooks.com

By purchasing this book you are eligible for one month membership to ForgottenBooks.com, giving you unlimited access to our entire collection of over 700,000 titles via our web site and mobile apps.

To claim your free month visit:
www.forgottenbooks.com/free285903

English
Français
Deutsche
Italiano
Español
Português

www.forgottenbooks.com

Mythology Photography **Fiction**
Fishing Christianity **Art** Cooking
Essays Buddhism Freemasonry
Medicine **Biology** Music **Ancient**
Egypt Evolution Carpentry Physics
Dance Geology **Mathematics** Fitness
Shakespeare **Folklore** Yoga Marketing
Confidence Immortality Biographies
Poetry **Psychology** Witchcraft
Electronics Chemistry History **Law**
Accounting **Philosophy** Anthropology
Alchemy Drama Quantum Mechanics
Atheism Sexual Health **Ancient History**
Entrepreneurship Languages Sport
Paleontology Needlework Islam
Metaphysics Investment Archaeology
Parenting Statistics Criminology
Motivational

THE CASSILIS ENGAGEMENT

A COMEDY IN FOUR ACTS

BY ST. JOHN HANKIN

LONDON

MARTIN SECKER PUBLISHER

NUMBER FIVE JOHN STREET ADELPHI

THE PERSONS OF THE COMEDY

Mrs. Cassilis

Geoffrey Cassilis (*her son*)

Lady Marchmont (*her sister*)

The Countess of Remenham

Major Warrington (*her brother*)

Lady Mabel Venning (*her daughter*)

Mrs. Borridge

Ethel Borridge (*her daughter*)

The Rev. Hildebrand Herries (*the rector*)

Mrs. Herries (*his wife*)

Watson (*Butler at Deynham*)

Dorset (*Mrs. Cassilis's maid*)

Two Footmen

The action of the play passes at Deynham Abbey Mrs. Cassilis's house in Leicestershire, Act I. in the Drawing-room, Act II. on the Lawn, Act III. in the Smoking-room and Act IV. in the Morning-room. One night passes between Acts I. and II. and between Acts III. and IV., one week between Acts II. and III.

Cast of the Original production before the Stage Society at the Imperial Theatre, London on Feb. 10th, 1907:—

Mrs. Cassilis	MISS EVELYN WEEDEN
Lady Marchmont	MISS GERTRUDE BURNETT
The Countess of Remenham	MISS FLORENCE HAYDEN
Mrs. Herries	MISS K. M. ROMSEY
Mrs. Borridge	MISS CLARE GREET
Lady Mabel Venning	MISS ISABEL ROLAND
Ethel Borridge	MISS MAUDI DARRELL
The Rector	MR. F. MORLAND
Major Warrington ...	MR. SAM SOTHERN
Geoffrey Cassilis	MR. LANGHORNE BURTON
Watson	MR. RALE HUTTON
Dorset	MISS MARGARET MACKENZIE

The Play produced by MISS MADGE McINTOSH.

THE CASSILIS ENGAGEMENT.

ACT I.

SCENE :—*The white drawing-room at Deynham Abbey, a very handsome room furnished in the Louis Seize style. There are big double doors at the back, and a large tea-table, with teacups etc. on cloth, stands rather to the left of it. There is a large French window open on the left of the stage, with a sofa in front of it facing the view. On the opposite side of the room is the fireplace, but there is no fire as the month is August. Two or three armchairs stand near it. When the curtain rises the RECTOR is standing judicially on hearthrug. He seems about to hum a tune, but thinks better of it. MRS. HERRIES is standing by window. Presently she crosses to her husband, and sits in one of the armchairs. The RECTOR is a rubicund, humorous-looking man of fifty; his wife a prosperous-looking lady a few years younger.*

MRS. HERRIES :

I wonder what can be keeping Mrs. Cassilis?

RECTOR
(*back to fire*) :

My dear, I told you we oughtn't to have called. On so sad an occasion——

MRS. HERRIES :

My dear Hildebrand, it's just on these sad occasions that a visit is so consoling. One should always call after a birth, a funeral——

BUTLER

(showing in LADY REMENHAM *and her daughter)*

I will tell Mrs. Cassilis you are here, my lady. She will be down in a moment.

LADY REMENHAM :

Thank you.   How do you do, Mrs. Herries? How do you do, Rector?

*(*LADY REMENHAM *goes towards fireplace and shakes hands. She is a dignified old lady of about sixty. Her normal expression is one of placid self-assurance, but to-day she has the air of disapproving of something or somebody.* MABEL *is a very pretty girl of two and twenty.* LADY REMENHAM *seats herself comfortably by* MRS. HERRIES. MABEL *goes over to window, where the* RECTOR *joins her.)*

MRS. HERRIES :

How do you do, Lady Remenham?

RECTOR :

How do you do, Mabel?

LADY REMENHAM :

You've heard this dreadful news, haven't you? *(*RECTOR *makes sympathetic gesture)*

MRS. HERRIES :

Yes.   Poor Mrs. Cassilis.

LADY REMENHAM :

Poor Adelaide, indeed!   That unhappy boy! But there!   How any mother can allow such a thing to happen passes my comprehension. To get engaged !

RECTOR
(*nods sympathetically*):

Just so.

LADY REMENHAM:

Engagements are such troublesome things. They sometimes even lead to marriage. But we'll hope it won't be as bad as that in this case. You've not heard who she is, I suppose?

MRS. HERRIES
(*shaking her head mournfully*):

No.

LADY REMENHAM:

Ah. Someone quite impossible, of course. Otherwise Adelaide would have told me in her letter.

MRS. HERRIES:

I'm afraid so.

LADY REMENHAM
(*irritably*):

It's really extremely wicked of Geoffrey. And so silly, too!—which is worse. A temporary infatuation I could understand, terminated by some small monetary payment. It would have been regrettable, of course, but young men are like that. And Adelaide could have stopped it out of his allowance. But an engagement! I am quite shocked at her.

MABEL
(*at window, turning to her mother*):

Don't you think, mamma, we might leave Mrs. Cassilis to manage her son's affairs her own way?

LADY REMENHAM:

She has *not* managed them. That's exactly what I complain of. I can't altogether acquit the Rector of some blame in the matter. He was Geoffrey's tutor for years. They used to say in *my* young days, " Train up a child in the way he should go ——"

RECTOR
(*attempting a mild jest*):

And when he's grown up he'll give you a great deal of anxiety. So they did! So they did!

LADY REMENHAM
(*severely*):

That is not the ending *I* remember.

RECTOR:

That is the Revised Version. (MRS. HERRIES *frowns. She feels this is not a moment for* levity)

LADY REMENHAM:

I dare say. They seem to alter everything nowadays. But, if so, I hardly see the use of education.

RECTOR
(*obstinately cheerful*):

I have long been of that opinion, Lady Remenham. (MRS. CASSILIS, *in a charming flutter of apologies, enters at this moment. She is a very pretty woman of forty, tall and graceful, and exquisitely dressed*)

Mrs. Cassilis :

You *must* forgive me all of you.   I had some letters to finish.   (*general handshake.   Kiss to* Mabel)   Dear Mabel.   How do you do, Mrs. Herries?

Rector :

How do you do, Mrs. Cassilis?

Lady Remenham :

My dear Adelaide, *what* a charming gown! But you always do have the most delightful clothes. Where *do* you get them?

Mrs. Cassilis :

Clarice made this.   (*two footmen bring the tea-table down into the middle of the room.   The* Butler, *who has brought in a teapot on a salver, places it on the table, and brings up a chair for* Mrs. Cassilis.   *The footmen go out*)

Lady Remenham :

Clarice?   The wretch!   She always makes my things atrociously.   If only I had your figure!

Mrs. Cassilis :

Excuse me, dear.   (*to* Butler)   The carriage has gone to the station to meet Lady Marchmont, Watson?

Butler :

Yes, madam.   It started five minutes ago.   (*exit* Butler)

MRS. CASSILIS
(*to* LADY REMENHAM):

I'm so glad you like it.   (*goes to tea-table and seats herself*)

LADY REMENHAM:
Is Margaret coming to stay with you?

MRS. CASSILIS:
Yes, for ten days.

LADY REMENHAM
(*drawing chair up to table*):

And now will you please pour out my tea?   I have come here to scold you, and I shall require several cups.

MRS. CASSILIS
(*quite cheerful*):

To scold *me?*   Won't you all bring your chairs to the table? (*they all do so*) Rector, where are you? (*to* LADY REMENHAM) Cream?

LADY REMENHAM:
Thank you.   And a small lump.

MRS. CASSILIS:
And why am I to be scolded?

LADY REMENHAM:
You know quite well. (*sternly*) Adelaide, what is this I hear about Geoffrey's engagement?

Mrs. Cassilis
(*not at all* disturbed) :

Oh, that? Yes, Geoffrey has got engaged to a girl in London. Isn't it romantic of him! I know nothing whatever about her except that I believe she has no money, and Geoffrey is over head and ears in love with her.

Mrs. Herries
(blandly) :

My dear Mrs. Cassilis, I should have thought *that* was quite enough!

Mrs. Cassilis :

Rector, will you cut that cake? It's just by your hand.

Lady Remenham
(*refusing to be diverted from the task of cross-examination*) :

Where did he meet her?

Mrs. Cassilis :

In an omnibus, I understand.

Lady Remenham
(*scandalised*) :

An omnibus!

Mrs. Cassilis :

Yes. That was so romantic, too! One of the horses fell down, and she was frightened. They thought she was going to faint. Geoffrey got her out, took charge of her, discovered her address, and

took her home.   Wasn't it clever of him?   Of
course, she asked him to come in.   He was introduced to her mother.   And now they're engaged.
(*gives cup* to RECTOR)

LADY REMENHAM
(*with awful* dignity) :

And what is the name of this young person?

MRS. CASSILIS :

Borridge.

LADY REMENHAM :

Borridge!   Mabel, my love, pray remember if
ever you come home and inform me that you
are engaged to a person of the name of Borridge I
shall whip you.   (*puts down cup*)

MABEL :

Very well, mamma.

MRS. CASSILIS :

Another cup?

LADY REMENHAM :

Thank you.   Rather less sugar this time.   (*gives
cup*)   I never could understand why you let Geoffrey
be in London at all.   Alone too.   Young men ought
never to be allowed out alone at his age.   They are
so susceptible.

MABEL :

Geoffrey has his profession, mamma.

MRS. CASSILIS :

Geoffrey's at the Bar, you know.

LADY REMENHAM :

The Bar! What business has Geoffrey to be at the Bar! Deynham has the best shooting in the Shires, and in the winter there's the hunting. What more does he want? It's disgraceful.

RECTOR
(*another mild effort at humour*) :

My dear Lady Remenham, you're sure you're not confusing the *Bar* with the *Dock?*

MRS. HERRIES :

Hildebrand!

LADY REMENHAM
(*impatiently*) :

The Bar is a good enough profession, of course. But only for very younger sons. Geoffrey will have Deynham some day, and twelve thousand a year. I don't think Adelaide need have made a little attorney of him.

MRS. CASSILIS :

Young men must do *something*, don't you think?

LADY REMENHAM
(*briskly*) :

Certainly not! It's this vulgar Radical notion that people ought to *do* things that is ruining English Society. What did Mr. Borridge *do*, by the way?

MRS. CASSILIS
(*hesitates*) :

He was a bookmaker, I believe.

LADY REMENHAM
(triumphantly):

There, you see! That's what comes of doing things!

MRS. CASSILIS
(slight shrug. Pouring herself out more tea, and still quite unruffled):

Well, I'm afraid there's no use in discussing it. They're engaged, and Miss Borridge is coming down here.

MRS. HERRIES:

Coming here!

LADY REMENHAM:

Coming here! ! !

MRS. CASSILIS:

Yes. On a visit. With her mother.

LADY REMENHAM
(putting down her cup with a touch of solemniiy):

Adelaide, are you—excuse my asking the question —are you quite in your right mind?

MRS. CASSILIS
(laughing):

I believe so.

LADY REMENHAM:

You've noticed nothing? No dizziness about the head? No singing in the ears? (MRS. CASSILIS shakes her head) And yet you ask this young woman to stay with you! And her mother! Neither of whom you know anything whatever about!

MRS. CASSILIS :

Another cup? (LADY REMENHAM *shakes her head irritably*)

LADY REMENHAM :

Is *Mr*. Borridge—Ugh!—coming too?

MRS. CASSILIS :

He is dead, I believe.

LADY REMENHAM :

That, at least, is satisfactory.

MABEL :

Mamma !

LADY REMENHAM :

Mabel, I shall do my duty whatever happens. (*turning to* MRS. CASSILIS *again*)   And does Mrs. Borridge carry on the business?   I think you said he was a boot-maker?

MABEL :

Book-maker.

MRS. CASSILIS
(*refusing to take offence*) :

No.   I believe he left her some small annuity.

LADY REMENHAM :

Annuity?   Ah, dies with her, of course?

MRS. CASSILIS :

No doubt.

LADY REMENHAM
(*gasps*) :

Well, Adelaide, I never should have believed it of
you.   To ask these people to the house !

MRS. CASSILIS :

Why shouldn't I ask them?.   Geoffrey tells me
Ethel is charming.

LADY REMENHAM :

Ethel?

MRS. CASSILIS :.

Miss Borridge.

LADY REMENHAM :

Bah ! (enter BUTLER, *showing in another visitor.
This is* LADY MARCHMONT, MRS. CASSILIS'S *sister.
She is a woman of about five-and-forty.   She wears
a light travelling cloak.   She is not unlike* MRS.
CASSILIS *in appearance and manner, but is of a
more delicate, fragile type*)

BUTLER :

Lady Marchmont.

MRS. CASSILIS
(rising) :

Ah, Margaret.   How glad I am to see you.
Some more tea, Watson.

LADY MARCHMONT
(*kisses her*) :

Not for me, please.   No, really.   My doctor
won't *hear* of it.   Hot water with a little milk is the

most he allows me. How do you do, dear? (*shaking hands with the* others) How do you do? How do you do? (BUTLER *goes out*)

MRS. CASSILIS :

How's the General?

LADY MARCHMONT :

Very gouty. His temper this morning was atrocions, poor man.

LADY REMENHAM
(*shakes her head*) :

You bear it like a saint, dear.

LADY MARCHMONT
(*philosophically,* sitting in *armchair after laying aside her* cloak) :

Yes—I go away a good deal. He finds my absence very soothing. That's why I was so glad to accept Adelaide's invitation when she asked me.

MRS. CASSILIS :

My dear, you'll be invaluable. I look to you to help me with my visitors.

LADY REMENHAM :

Poor Margaret. But you always were so unselfish.

LADY MARCHMONT :

Are they very——?

LADY REMENHAM :

Very.

MRS. CASSILIS
(*laughing*):

My dear, Lady Remenham knows nothing whatever about them.

LADY REMENHAM
(*firmly*):

I know everything about them.   The girl has no
money.   She has no position.   She became engaged
to Geoffrey without your knowledge.   She has a
perfectly dreadful mother.   And her name is Borridge.

LADY MARCHMONT
(raising *her* brows):

When are they coming?

MRS. CASSILIS.

I expect them in half an hour.   The carriage was
to go straight back to the station to meet them.

LADY REMENHAM
(*ruffling her feathers angrily*):

I hope Geoffrey is conscious of the folly and wick-
edness of his conduct.

LADY MARCHMONT:

Where is he, dear?

MRS. CASSILIS:

He's down here with me—and as happy as possible, I'm glad to say.

LADY REMENHAM:

Extraordinary! But the young men of the present day *are* extraordinary. Young men nowadays
seem always to be either irreclaimably vicious or
deplorably silly. I prefer them vicious. They give
less trouble. My poor brother Algernon—you remember Algernon, don't you, Rector? He was another of your pupils .

RECTOR
(*sighs*):

Yes, I remember.

MRS. HERRIES:

Major Warrington hasn't been down for quite a
long time, has he?

LADY REMENHAM.

No. We don't ask him to Milverton now. He
comes to us in London, but in the country one has
to be more particular. He really is dreadfully dissipated. Always running after some petticoat or
other. Often more than one. But there is safety
in numbers, don't you think?

RECTOR:

Unquestionably.

LADY REMENHAM:

Algernon always says he is by temperament a
polygamist. I don't know what he means. However, I've no anxiety about *him*. *He never* gets engaged. He's far too *clever* for that. I wonder if
he could help you out of this dreadful entanglement?
In a case of this kind one should have the very best
advice.

Mrs. Cassilis
(laughing) :

I shall be delighted to see Major Warrington—
though not for the reason you suggest.

Lady Remenham :

Well, I'll ask him down.   Remenham won't like
it.   He disapproves of him so much.   He gets quite
virtuous about it.   But that sort of moral indignation should never be allowed to get out of hand,
should it?   (Rector nods)   Besides, he's away
just now.   I'll write to Algernon directly I get back,
and I'll bring him over to dinner one day next week.
Say Thursday?

Lady Marchmont :

Do, dear.   I adore Major Warrington.

Lady Remenham :

I dare say.   *(preparing to go)*   He's not your
brother.   Meantime, I can ask him whether he
knows anything against Mrs. Borridge.   But he's
sure to.   He knows nearly all the detrimental people in London, especially if their daughters are in
the least attractive.

Mrs. ˙Cassilis
(smiling) :

You'll come *with* him on Thursday, won't you?
And Mabel?   (Mabel rises)

Lady Remenham :

Perhaps that will be best.   Then I can keep my
brother within bounds.   Poor Algernon is apt to

take too much champagne unless I am there to prevent him. And now, dear, I really must go. (*she
and* MABEL *go up towards* door) Good-bye.

MRS. CASSILIS :

You won't stay to meet Mrs. Borridge?

LADY REMENHAM
(*shudders*) :

I think not. Thursday will be q*uite* soon enough.
Good-bye, Mrs. Herries. (*as they reach door*
GEOFFREY *opens it, and almost runs into her arms*)
Ah, *here* is the young man who is causing us all this
distress.

GEOFFREY :

I, Lady Remenham? (*shakes hands*) How do
you do, Aunt Margaret? (*shakes hands with
others*)

LADY REMENHAM
(*shakes hands*) :

You. What do you *mean* by getting engaged to
someone we none of us know anything about?

MABEL :

Mamma !

LADY REMENHAM :

I consider your conduct perfectly heartless. Its
Joolishness needs no comment from me.

GEOFFREY :

Really, Lady Remenham——

LADY REMENHAM :

Tut, tut, sir. Don't " really " me. I'm ashamed
of you. And now I'll be off before I quarrel with
you. Come, Mabel. (*sweeps out, followed* by
MABEL. GEOFFREY *opens door for them, and then
takes them down to their carriage*)

MRS. HERRIES :

I think we ought to be going, too. Come, Hildebrand. (*shakes hands*)

(MRS. CASSILIS *rings.*)

RECTOR :

Good-bye, Mrs. Cassilis. Let's hope everything
will turn out for the best.

MRS. HERRIES :

It never does. Good-bye.

MRS. CASSILIS
(*going towards door with* RECTOR) :

Good-bye. (*shakes hands warmly*) And you'll
both come and dine on Thursday, won't you? To-
morrow week that is. Major Warrington will want
to see his old tutor.

RECTOR :

You're very good. (*he and* MRS. HERRIES *go
out*)

MRS. CASSILIS
(*returning to her sister*) :

Dear Lady Remenham! What nonsense she
talks.

LADY MARCHMONT:

People who talk as much as that must talk a good deal of nonsense, mustn't they? Otherwise they'd have nothing to say. (*re-enter* GEOFFREY)

GEOFFREY:

Lady Remenham seems ruffled.

LADY MARCHMONT:

About your engagement? I'm not surprised.

GEOFFREY:

I don't see what it's got to do with her.

LADY MARCHMONT:

You must make allowance for a mother's feelings, my dear Geoffrey.

GEOFFREY

(*pats* MRS. CASSILIS'S *hand, then goes to tea-table and helps himself to tea*):

Lady Remenham isn't my mother. She's my god-mother.

LADY MARCHMONT:

She's Mabel's mother.

MRS. CASSILIS:

Sh! Margaret.

LADY MARCHMONT:

My dear, there's no use making mysteries about things. Geoffrey was always supposed to be going to marry Mabel ever since they were children. He knows that.

GEOFFREY :

That was only boy and girl talk.

LADY MARCHMONT :

For you, perhaps.

GEOFFREY :

And for her. Mabel never expected—— (*pause.
He thinks*)

LADY MARCHMONT :

Did you ever ask her?

GEOFFREY :

But I never supposed——

LADY MARCHMONT :

I think you *should* have supposed. A boy should
be very careful how he encourages a girl to think
of him in that way.

GEOFFREY :

But I'd no idea. Of course, I like Mabel. I
like her awfully. We're like brother and sister.
But beyond that—— (*pause*) Mother, do *you*
think I've behaved badly to Mabel?

MRS. CASSILIS
(gently) :

I think perhaps you've a little disappointed her.

GEOFFREY
(*peevishly*) :

Why didn't somebody *tell* me? How was I to
know?

LADY MARCHMONT:

My dear boy, we couldn't be expected to know you were absolutely blind.

MRS. CASSILIS:

Margaret, you're not to scold Geoffrey. I won't allow it.

GEOFFREY:

Mother, dear—you won't allow this to make any difference? With Ethel, I mean?

MRS. CASSILIS:

Of course not, Geoff. (lays hand on his)

GEOFFREY
(earnestly) :

She's so fond of me. And I'm so fond of her. We were made for each other. I couldn't bear it if you were unkind to her.

MRS. CASSILIS:

My dear Geoff. I'm sure Ethel is everything that is sweet and good, or my boy wouldn't love her. And I intend to fall in love with her myself directly I set eyes on her.

GEOFFREY :

Dear mother! (pats her hand affectionately. Pause; then, thoughtfully) I'm afraid you'll find her mother rather trying—at first. She's not quite a lady, you know. . . . But she's very good-natured.

MRS. CASSILIS
(*cheerfully*) :

Well, well, we shall see.   And now run away, dear, and leave me to talk to Margaret, and I'll undertake that all symptoms of crossness shall have disappeared before our visitors arrive.

GEOFFREY :

All right, mother.   (*kisses her and goes out*)

LADY MARCHMONT
(*looking after him reflectively*) :

How you spoil that boy !

MRS. CASSILIS
(*lightly*) :

What else should I do with him? He's my only one.   Mothers always spoil their sons, don't they? And quarrel with their daughters.   More marriages are due to girls being unhappy at home than most people imagine.

LADY MARCHMONT :

And yet Geoffrey wants to leave you, apparently.

MRS. CASSILIS
(*smiling bravely; but her eyes have a suspicion of moisture in them*) :

Evidently I didn't spoil him enough.

LADY MARCHMONT
(*washing her hands of the whole affair*) :

Well, I'm glad you're pleased with this engagement.

Mrs. Cassilis

(*sudden change of manner. Her face loses its brightness, and she suddenly seems to look older*):
Pleased with it! Do you really believe that?

Lady Marchmont:

Didn't you say so?

Mrs. Cassilis
(*shrugs*):

To Lady Remenham and Mrs. Herries. Yes.

Lady Marchmont:

And to Geoffrey.

Mrs. Cassilis:

And Geoffrey, too. (*half to herself*) Mothers can't always be straightforward with their sons, can they?

Lady Marchmont:

Why not?
(*There is a pause while* Mrs. Cassilis *makes up her mind whether to answer this or not. Then she seems to decide to speak out. She moves nearer to her sister, and when she begins her voice is very firm and matter-of-fact.*)

Mrs. Cassilis:

My dear Margaret, what would *you* do if your son suddenly wrote to you that he had become engaged to a girl you knew nothing whatever about, a girl far beneath him in social rank?

LADY MARCHMONT
(*firmly*) :

I should forbid the engagement. Forbid it absolutely.

MRS. CASSILIS :

Without seeing the girl?

LADY MARCHMONT :

Certainly. The mere fact of her accepting my son before I had ever set eyes on her would have been quite enough.

MRS. CASSILIS :

But supposing your son were of age and independent?

LADY MARCHMONT
(*impatiently*) :

Geoffrey isn't independent.

MRS. CASSILIS :

He has five hundred a year.

LADY MARCHMONT
(*contemptuously*) :

What's *that?*

MRS. CASSILIS :

Besides, Geoffrey knows I should always be willing to help him.

LADY MARCHMONT :

That's just it. He ought *not* to have known. You ought to have made it clear to him from the first that if he married without your consent he would never have a penny from you, either now or at your death. Deynham isn't entailed, fortunately.

MRS. CASSILIS:

But, my dear, I couldn't *disinherit* Geoffrey! How could I?

LADY MARCHMONT
(*shrugs*):

You could have threatened to. And then the girl wouldn't have accepted him.

MRS. CASSILIS:

I don't know. (*thoughtfully*) Five hundred a year may seem a considerable sum to her.

LADY MARCHMONT
(*horrified*):

Is it as bad as that?

MRS. CASSILIS
(*trying to smile*):

Besides, she may be really in love with him.

LADY MARCHMONT
(*snappish*):

What *has* that to do with it?

MRS. CASSILIS:

Young people. In love. They are seldom prudent, are they?

LADY MARCHMONT

Still, I should have forbidden the engagement.

MRS. CASSILIS :

And then?

LADY MARCHMONT :

What do you mean?

MRS. CASSILIS :

If Geoffrey had defied me? Boys can be very obstinate.

LADY MARCHMONT :

I should have refused ever to see him again.

MRS. CASSILIS :

Ah, Margaret, I couldn't do that. Geoffrey is everything I have. He is my only son, my joy and my pride. I couldn't quarrel with him whatever happened. (LADY MARCHMONT leans back with gesture of impatience) No, Margaret, my plan was the best.

LADY MARCHMONT :

What *is* your plan?

MRS. CASSILIS
(quite *practical*) :

My plan is to give the thing a fair trial. Ask her down here. Ask her mother down here. And see what happens.

LADY MARCHMONT
(looking *at her* narrowly) :

Nothing else?

MRS. CASSILIS :

Nothing else—at present.

LADY MARCHMONT :

You could have done that without sanctioning
the engagement.

MRS. CASSILIS :

Yes. But love thrives on opposition. There's a
fascination about a runaway match. It has
romance. Whereas there's no romance at all about
an ordinary wedding. It's only dull and rather vulgar. (wearily) And, after all, the girl may be
presentable.

LADY MARCHMONT :

Borridge! (crisply) I'm not very sanguine
about that.

MRS. CASSILIS :

Anyhow, she's pretty, and Geoffrey loves her.
That's all we know about her at present.

LADY MARCHMONT :

Wretched boy. To think he should have allowed
himself to be caught in this way! . . . Don't
you think you might have asked the daughter without the mother?

MRS. CASSILIS :

So Geoffrey suggested. He seemed rather nervous about having her here. She's rather a terrible
person, I gather. But I said as we were marrying

into the family we mustn't be unkind to her. (*with a slow smile*) Poor boy, he rather blenched at that. I think he hadn't associated *Mrs.* Borridge with his matrimonial schemes. It's just as well he should do so at once, don't you think?

BUTLER :

Mrs. and Miss Borridge. (*enter* MRS. BORRIDGE *and* ETHEL)

(*Both rise. LADY MARCHMONT turns sharp round to look at the newcomers. MRS. CASSILIS goes up to meet them with her sweetest smile. Nothing could be more hospitable than her manner or more gracious than her welcome. The change from the MRS. CASSILIS of a moment before, with the resolute set of the lips and the glitter in the eyes, to this gentle, caressing creature, does the greatest credit to her powers of self-control. LADY MARCHMONT notices it, and is a little shocked.*)

MRS. CASSILIS :

How do you do? *How* do you do, my dear? (*kisses* ETHEL) Tell Mr. Geoffrey, Watson. I hope you've not had a tiring journey, Mrs. Borridge? (*exit* BUTLER)

MRS. BORRIDGE :

Not at all, Mrs. Cassilis. We 'ad—had—the compartment to ourselves, bein' first class. As I says to my girlie, " They'll very likely send the carridge to meet us, and it looks better for the servants."

(*MRS. BORRIDGE comes down stage. She is a large, gross woman, rather over-dressed in inexpensive materials. Too much colour in her hat and far too much in her cheeks. But a beaming, good-natured harridan for all that. As a landlady you would rather like her. She smiles nervously in* LADY MARCHMONT'S *direction, not sure whether she ought to say anything or wait to be introduced. Her daughter keeps by her side, watching to see she doesn't commit herself, and quite sure that she will.* ETHEL *is pretty but second-rate, but has had the sense to dress simply, and therefore is less appallingly out of the picture than her far more amiable mother.)*

MRS. CASSILIS :

Let me introduce you. Mrs. Borridge—Lady Marchmont, Miss Borridge. (LADY MARCHMONT *bows*)

MRS. BORRIDGE
(extends gloved hand) :

How do you do, Lady Marchmont? Proud, I'm sure.

*(*LADY MARCHMONT *finds nothing to say, and for the moment there is a constrained pause. Then enter* GEOFFREY *hurriedly.)*

GEOFFREY
(with as much heartiness as he can muster, but it rings a little hollow) :

How do you do, Mrs. Borridge? Ethel, dear, how long have you been here? I didn't hear you come? *(kisses her)*

ETHEL :

We've only just got here.

MRS. BORRIDGE
(*subsiding* into *an armchair*) :

Don't apologise, Geoffy. Your ma's been entertaining us most kind.

GEOFFREY
(*with look of gratitude to* MRS. CASSILIS) :
Dear mother.

MRS. BORRIDGE :
Well, how *are* you, Geoffy? You look first-rate.

GEOFFREY :
Oh, I'm all right.

MRS. BORRIDGE :
And what a fine 'ouse—house—you've got! Quit
a palace I declare!

GEOFFREY :
I'm glad you like it.

MRS. BORRIDGE :
And it'll all be yours some day. Won't it?

ETHEL
(*pulls her sleeve*) :
Mother!

GEOFFREY :
That's as my mother decides.

MRS. BORRIDGE :
Then you're sure to 'ave it. I know what
mothers are! And what a 'andsome room, too.
Quite like the Metropole at Brighton.   (enter MRS.

Cassilis's *maid. She is* in *a perfectly plain black dress, and looks enormously more like a lady than* Ethel)

MAID :

Can I have your keys, madam?

MRS. BORRIDGE
(*surprised*) :

My keys?

MAID :

The keys of your trunks, madam.

MRS. BORRIDGE :

Certainly not. Who ever 'eard of such a thing?

MAID :

I thought you might wish me to unpack for you, madam.

MRS. BORRIDGE
(bristling) :

Oh. *Did* you! I don't want no strange girls ferriting in *my* boxes. (ETHEL nudges *her arm*) What *is* it, Eth? Oh, very well. But I'm not going to let her all the same. No, thank you.

MRS. CASSILIS
(quite *self-possessed.* LADY MARCHMONT *nervously avoids her eye*) :

Mrs. Borridge will unpack for herself, Dorset. (MAID bows, *and turns to go out*) Wait a moment. (MAID *pauses at door*) Would you like to take off your things at once, Mrs. Borridge? If so, Dorset shall show you your room. And I'll have some tea

sent up to you there.   You'll want it after your
journey. (*feels teapot*) This is quite cold.   What
do you say, Ethel?

ETHEL :

Thank you, Mrs. Cassilis.   A cup of tea would
be very nice.

MRS. CASSILIS :

Show Mrs. Borridge her room, Dorset.   (MRS.
BORRIDGE *rises*) And take her up some tea.   Dinner will be at eight.   You'll ring if there's anything
you want, won't you?

MRS. BORRIDGE :

Thank you, Mrs. Cassilis.

(MRS. BORRIDGE *waddles out, beaming. She feels
that her first introduction to the houses of the great
has gone off successfully.   GEOFFREY holds the
door open for them, and gives ETHEL a sly kiss in
passing.   MRS. CASSILIS makes no sign, but one
can feel her shudder at the sound.   GEOFFREY
comes down to her a moment later, brimming with
enthusiasm.*)

GEOFFREY :

Well, mother *what* do you think of her?   Isn't
she *sweet?*

MRS. CASSILIS
(*gently*) :

She's very pretty, Geoff. (*lays hand on his*)

GEOFFREY :

And *good!* You don't know how *good* she is !

Mrs. Cassilis :

So long as she's good to my boy that's all I ask.

Geoffrey :

Dearest mother. (*kisses her demonstratively*) Now I'll go and dress. (*goes out quickly, with a boyish feeling that he has been rather too demonstrative for a true-born Englishman*)

Lady Marchmont

(*There is a long pause, during which* Lady Marchmont *looks at her sister,* Mrs. Cassilis *at nothing The latter is evidently in deep thought, and seems to have almost forgotten her sister's presence. At last* Lady Marchmont *speaks with the stern accent of " I told you so."*)

And that's the girl your son is to marry.

Mrs. Cassilis :

Marry her ! Nonsense, my dear Margaret.
(*The curtain falls.*)

ACT II.

Scene :—*The lawn at Deynham. Time, after breakfast the following morning. Under a tree stand two or three long wicker chairs, with bright red cushions. On the right stands the house, with windows open on to the terrace. A path on the left leads to the flower garden, and another on the*

*same side to the strawberry beds.   When the
curtain rises, MRS. CASSILIS comes on to the terrace, followed by ETHEL, and a little later by MRS.
BORRIDGE.   The last-named is flushed with food,
and gorgeously arrayed in a green silk blouse.
She is obviously in the best of spirits, and is generally terribly at ease in Zion.*

MRS. CASSILIS :

Shall we come out on the lawn?   It's such a perfect morning.

ETHEL :

That *will* be jolly, Mrs. Cassilis.   (t*hey come
down*)   When I'm in the country I shall always eat
too much breakfast and then spend the morning on
a long chair digesting it.   So will mother.

MRS. BORRIDGE :

How you go on, dearie !

MRS. CASSILIS :

Try this chair, then.   (*slightly moving long chair
forward*)   Mrs. Borridge, what kind of chair do *you*
like?

MRS. BORRIDGE :

This'll do.   I'm not particular.   (*subsides into
another long chair*)   Am I showing my ankles, Eth?

ETHEL :

Sh ! mother !   (*giggles*)

MRS. BORRIDGE :

Well, I only asked, dearie.

MRS. CASSILIS :

I wonder if you'd like a cushion for your head?
Try this. (*puts vivid red cushion behind* MRS.
BORRIDGE'S *vivid green blouse. The effect is electrifying*)

MRS. BORRIDGE :

That's better. (MRS. CASSILIS *sinks negligently
in wicker chair and puts up white lace parasol*)

ETHEL
(*sigh of* content) :

I call this Heaven, Mrs. Cassilis.

MRS. CASSILIS :

That's right, my dear. Are you fond of the
country?

ETHEL :

I don't know. I've never been there so far. Not
to the real country, I mean. Mums and I have a
week at Brighton now and then. And once we went
for a month to Broadstairs after I had the measles.
But that's not exactly country, is it?

MRS. CASSILIS :

You're sure to like it. Geoffrey loves it. He's
never so happy as when he's pottering about Deynham with his gun.

ETHEL :

Doesn't he get tired of that?

MRS. CASSILIS :

Oh, no. Besides, he doesn't do that all the year

round. He rides a great deal. We've very good hunting at Deynham. Are you fond of horses?

ETHEL :

I can't bear them, Mrs. Cassilis.

MRS. BORRIDGE :

When she was a little tot her father put 'er—her —on a pony and she fell off. It didn't hurt 'er, but the doctor said 'er nerve was shook. And now she can't bear 'orses.

MRS. CASSILIS :

What a pity! I do hope you won't be dull while you're with us. Perhaps you're fond of walking?

ETHEL :

Yes. I don't mind walking—for a little. If there's anything to walk *to*.

MRS. CASSILIS :

We often walk up Milverton Hill on fine afternoons to see the view. It's the highest point about here.

ETHEL
(*stifling a yawn*) :

Is it, Mrs. Cassilis?

MRS. CASSILIS :

And no doubt we shall find other things to amuse you. What *do* you like?

ETHEL :

Oh, shops and theatres, and lunching at restaurants and dancing, and, oh, lots of things.

MRS. CASSILIS:

I'm afraid we've no shops nearer than Leicester, and that's twelve miles away. And we've no restaurants at all. But I dare say we could get up a dance for you.

ETHEL
(clapping her hands):

That'll be *sweet!* I simply *love* dancing. And all the rest of the time I shall sit on the lawn and grow fat, like mummy. (protest from MRS. BORRIDGE) Oh, yes, I shall.

MRS. BORRIDGE:

Ethel, don't be saucy.

ETHEL
(laughing):

Mummy, if you scold me you'll have to go in. It's far too hot to be scolded.

MRS. BORRIDGE:

Isn't she a spoilt girl, Mrs. Cassilis? What they taught you at that boarding school, miss, I don't know. Not manners, *I* can see.

ETHEL
(ruffling her mother's wig):

There! there! mums. Was 'em's cross?

MRS. BORRIDGE
(pettishly):

Stop it, Ethel, stop it, I say. Whatever will Mrs. Cassilis think of you!

MRS. CASSILIS
(*smiling sweetly*) :

Don't scold her, Mrs. Borridge.   It's so pleasant to see a little high spirits, isn't it?

MRS. BORRIDGE
(*beaming*) :

Well, if *you* don't mind, Mrs. Cassilis, *I* don't. But it's not the way girls were taught to behave in *my* young days.

ETHEL
(*slight yawn*) :

That was so long ago, mums!

MRS. CASSILIS
(*rising*) :

Well, I must go and see after my housekeeping. Can you entertain each other while I'm away for a little?   My sister will be down soon, I hope.   She had breakfast in her room.   And Geoffrey will be back in half an hour.   I asked him to ride over to Milverton for me with a note.

ETHEL :

We shall be all right, Mrs. Cassilis.   Mother'll go to sleep.   She always does if you make her too comfortable.   And then she'll snore, won't you, mums? (MRS. CASSILIS *goes into the house, smiling bravely to the last*)

MRS. BORRIDGE
(*alarmed*) :

Ethel, you shouldn't talk like that before Mrs. Cassilis.   She won't like it.

ETHEL:

Oh, yes she will. And I'm going to make her like *me* awfully. What lovely clothes she has! I wish *you* had lovely clothes, mums.

MRS. BORRIDGE:

What's the matter with my clothes, dearie? I 'ad on my best silk last night. And I bought this blouse special in the Grove only a week ago so as to do you credit.

ETHEL:

I know. Still . . . Couldn't you have chosen something quieter?

MRS. BORRIDGE:

Oh, no, dearie. I 'ate quiet things.

ETHEL:

Hate, mother.

MRS. BORRIDGE:

Hate, then. Give me something cheerful.

ETHEL
(hopelessly):

Very well, mummy.

MRS. BORRIDGE
(imploring):

But *do* be careful what you say before Mrs. Casilis. She's not used to girls being so free.

ETHEL:

Oh, yes she is, mums. All girls are like that nowadays. All girls that are ladies, I mean. They bet, and talk slang, and smoke cigarettes, and play bridge.   I know all about that.   I've read about it in the "Ladies' Mail."   One of them put ice down her young man's back at dinner, and when he broke off his engagement she only laughed.

MRS. BORRIDGE
(*lamentably*) :

Oh, dear, I do hope there won't be ice for dinner to-night.

ETHEL
(*laughing*) :

Poor mums, don't be anxious.   I'll be *very* careful, I promise you.

MRS. BORRIDGE
(*lamentably*) :

You're so 'eadstrong.   And I *do* want to see you married and respectable.   I wasn't always respectable myself, and I know what it means for a girl. Your sister Nan, she's gay, she is.   She 'adn't no ambition.   An' look what she is now !

ETHEL
(*looking round nervously*) :

If Geoff were to hear of it !

MRS. BORRIDGE :

'E won't.   Not 'e !   I've seen to that.

ETHEL :

These things always get known somehow.

MRS. BORRIDGE:

Nan's changed 'er name.   Calls 'erself Mrs.
Seymour.   An' she never comes to see us now.   If
she did, I'd show 'er the door fast enough.   Dis-
gracin' us like that!

ETHEL:

Poor Nan!

MRS. BORRIDGE
(*warmly*):

Don't you pity 'er.   She don't deserve it.   She
treated us like dirt.   She's a bad 'un all through.
I've done things myself as I didn't ought to 'ave
done.   But I've always *wanted* to be respectable.
But it's not so easy when you've your living to make
and no one to look to.   (ETHEL *nods*)   Yes, I've 'ad
my bad times, dearie.   But I've pulled through
them.   And I *made* your father marry me.   No one
can deny that.   It wasn't easy.   An' I had to give
him all my savings before e'd say " Yes."   And
even then I wasn't 'appy till we'd been to church.
But 'e did marry me in the end.   An' then *you* was
born, an' I says my girl shall be brought up respectable.   She shall be a lady.   And some day, when
she's married an' ridin' in her carriage, she'll say,
" It's all mother's doing."   (*wipes her eyes in
pensive melancholy*)

ETHEL:

How long *were* you married to father, mums?

MRS. BORRIDGE:

Only eight years, dearie.   Before that I was 'is
'ousekeeper.

ETHEL :

His, mummy.

MRS. BORRIDGE :

Very well, dearie. (*with quiet satisfaction*)
Father drank 'isself to death the year Ben d'or won
the Ledger. (*shaking her head*) He lost a pot o'
money over that, and it preyed on 'is mind. So he
took to the drink. If he 'adn't insured 'is life an'
kep' the premiums payed we should 'ave been in
the 'ouse, that's where we should 'ave been, dearie.

ETHEL :

Poor dad !

MRS. BORRIDGE :

Yes. 'E 'ad 'is faults. But 'e was a kind-
'earted man, was Joe Borridge. 'E died much re-
spected. (*cheering up*) An' now you're engaged to
a *real* gentleman ! *That's* the sort for my Eth !

ETHEL :

Oh ! sh ! mums. (*looking round nervously*)

MRS. BORRIDGE :

No one'll hear. And if they do, what's the harm?
You've got 'is promise.

ETHEL :

His, mother.

MRS. BORRIDGE :

You can hold 'im—him—to it.

ETHEL
(nodding) :

Yes. Besides, Geoff's awfully in love with me.
And I really rather like *him*, you know—in a way.

MRS. BORRIDGE :

I know, dearie. Still, I'd get something from
'im on paper if I was you, something that'll 'old
'im. The men takes a bit of 'olding nowadays.
They're that slippy! You get something that'll
'old 'im. That's what I always say to girls. Letters is best. Oh, the chances I've seen missed
through not gettin' something on paper!

ETHEL
(confidently) :

You needn't worry, mummy. Geoff's all right.

MRS. BORRIDGE :

I dare say. Still, I'd like something the lawyers
can take hold of. Geoffy may get tired of *you*,
dearie. Men are that changeable. *I* know them!

ETHEL
(viciously) :

He'd better not! I'd make him *pay* for it!

MRS. BORRIDGE :

So you could, dearie, if you 'ad somethin' on
paper. (ETHEL *shrugs impatiently*) Well, if you
won't, you won't. But if anythin' happens don't
say I didn't warn you, that's all. (*sighs*) I wish Geoffy was
a lord, like Lord Buckfastleigh,

ETHEL :

I don't.

MRS. BORRIDGE :

Well, not *just* like Buckfastleigh, per'aps.   But still, a lord.   You never did like Buckfastleigh.

ETHEL :

That old beast !

MRS. BORRIDGE
(*remonstrating*) :

He's been a good friend to us, dearie.   And he is an earl whatever you may say.

ETHEL :

Pah !

MRS. BORRIDGE :

And he's rich.   Richer than Geoffy.   And he's awfully sweet on you, dearie.   I believe he'd 'ave married you if 'is old woman 'ad turned up 'er toes last autumn.   And he's seventy-three.   He wouldn't 'ave lasted long.

ETHEL
(*fiercely*) :

I wouldn't marry him if he were twice as rich— and twice as old.

MRS. BORRIDGE
(*placidly*) :

I dare say you're right, dearie.   He's a queer 'un is Buckfastleigh.   But he offered to settle five thousand down if you'd go to Paris with 'im.   Five thousand down on the nail.   He wasn't what you'd call

sober when he said it, but he meant it.   I dare say
he'd 'ave made it seven if you hadn't boxed 'is ears.
(ETHEL *laughs*)   Wasn't I savage when you did
that, dearie!   But you was right 'as it turned out.
For Geoffy proposed next day.   And now you'll be a
real married woman.   There's nothing like being
married. It's so respectable.   When you're married you can look down on people.   And that's what
every woman wants.   That's why I pinched and
screwed and sent you to boarding school.   I said
my girlie shall be a real lady.   And she is.   (*much
moved at the reflection*)

ETHEL:

Is she, mums?

MRS. BORRIDGE:

Of   course,   dearie.   That's   why   she's   'ere.
Deynham Abbey, *two* footmen in livery, fire in 'er
bedroom, evenin' dress every night of 'er life. *Lady*
Marchmont invited to meet her!   Everythin' tip
top!   And it's not a bit too good for my girl.   It's
what she was made for.

ETHEL
(*thoughtfully*):

I wish Johnny Travers had had some money.
Then I could have married him.

MRS. BORRIDGE:

Married 'im—him!   Married a auctioneer's clerk
without twopence to bless 'isself.   I should think
not indeed!   Not likely!

ETHEL:

Still, I was awfully gone on Johnny.

MRS. BORRIDGE
(decidedly):

Nonsense, Eth.   I should 'ope we can look 'igher than *that!*

ETHEL:

Sh! mother.   Here's Geoff.
(GEOFFREY, *in riding breeches, comes out of the house.*)

GEOFFREY:

Good morning, dear.   (*kisses* ETHEL)   I thought I should be back earlier, but I rode over to Milverton for the mater.   (to MRS. BORRIDGE)   Good morning.

MRS. BORRIDGE
(archly):

You 'aven't no kisses to spare for *me*, 'ave you, Geoffy?   Never mind.   You keep 'em all for my girl.   She's worth 'em.

GEOFFREY
(caressing *her hand*):

Dear Ethel.

MRS. BORRIDGE:

How well you look in those riding togs, Geoffy!   Don't 'e Eth?   (*endeavouring to hoist herself out of her chair*)

ETHEL
(smiling at *him*):

Geoff always looks well in everything.

MRS. BORRIDGE :

Well, I'll go indoors and leave you two to spoon.
That's what you want, I know. I'll go and talk to
your ma. (*waddles off* into *the house, beaming*)

GEOFFREY
(*picking* rose *and* bringing *it to* ETHEL) :

A rose for the prettiest girl in England.

ETHEL :

Oh, Geoff, do you think so?

GEOFFREY :

Of course. The prettiest and the best. (*takes
her hand*)

ETHEL :

You do really love me, Geoff, don't you?

GEOFFREY :

Do you doubt it? (*kisses her*)

ETHEL :

No; you're much too good to me, you know.

GEOFFREY :

Nonsense, darling.

ETHEL :

It's the truth. You're a gentleman and rich, and
have fine friends. While mother and I are common
as common.

GEOFFREY
(*firmly*) :

You're *not*.

ETHEL :

Oh, yes we are. Of course, I've been to school, and been taught things. But what's education? It can't alter how we're made, can it? And she and I are the same underneath.

GEOFFREY :

Ethel, you're not to say such things, or to think them.

ETHEL :

But they're true, Geoff.

GEOFFREY :

They're *not*. (*kisses her*) Say they're not.

ETHEL
(*shakes her head*) :

No.

GEOFFREY :

Say they're *not*. (*kisses her*) *Not!*

ETHEL :

Very well. They're not.

GEOFFREY :

That's right. (*kiss*) There's a reward.

ETHEL
(*pulling herself away*) :

I wonder if I did right to say " Yes " when you asked me, Geoff? Right for *you*, I mean.

GEOFFREY :

Of course you did, darling. You love me, don't you?

ETHEL :

But wouldn't it have been best for you if I'd said " No "? Then you'd have married Lady Somebody or other, with lots and lots of money, and lived happy ever afterwards.

GEOFFREY
(indignantly) :

I shouldn't.

ETHEL :

Oh, yes, you would.

GEOFFREY :

And what would *you* have done, pray?

ETHEL :

Oh, I should have taken up with someone else, or perhaps married old Buckfastleigh when his wife died.

GEOFFREY :

Ethel !

ETHEL :

I should. I'm not the sort to go on moping for long. I should have been awfully down for a bit, and missed you every day. But by and by I should have cheered up and married someone else. I could have done it. I could !

GEOFFREY :

And what about *me?*

ETHEL:

Wouldn't you have been happier in the end, Geoff? I'm not the sort of wife you ought to have married. Some day I expect you'll come to hate me. (*sighs*) Heigho.

GEOFFREY

(*softly*):

You know I shan't, dear.

ETHEL:

But I did so want to marry a gentleman. Mother wanted it, too. (quite *simply*) So I said " Yes," you see.

GEOFFREY

(*drawing her to him*):

Darling! (*kisses her* tenderly)

ETHEL:

Geoff, what did your mother say when you told her we were engaged? Was she dreadfully down about it?

GEOFFREY:

No.

ETHEL:

On your honour?

GEOFFREY:

On my honour. Mother never said a single word to me against it. Lady Marchmont scolded me a bit. She's my aunt, you see.

ETHEL:

Old cat!

GEOFFREY :

And so did Lady Remenham. She's my god-
mother. But mother stood up for us all through.

ETHEL
(*sighs*) :

I shall never get on with all your fine friends,
Geoff.

GEOFFREY :

You will. Anyone who's as pretty as my Ethel
can get on anywhere.

ETHEL :

Yes, I *am* pretty, aren't I? I'm glad of that.
It makes a difference, doesn't it?

GEOFFREY :

Of course. In a week you'll have them all running after you.

ETHEL
(*clapping her hands*) :

Shall I, Geoff? Won't that be splendid! (*kisses
him*) Oh, Geoff, I'm so happy. When shall we
be married?

GEOFFREY :

I'm afraid not till next year, dear. Next June
mother says.

ETHEL
(*pouting*) :

That's a *long* way off, Geoff.

GEOFFREY :

Yes, but mother says you're to be here a *great*
deal between now and then, almost all the time, in
fact. So it won't be so bad, will it?

ETHEL :

Why does your mother want it put off till then?

GEOFFREY :

Something about the London season, she said.
We shall be married in London, of course, because
your mother's house is there.

ETHEL :

Oh, yes, of course.

GEOFFREY :

And besides, mother says she never believes in
very short engagements. She says girls sometimes don't quite know their own minds. I said I was
sure *you* weren't like that. But she asked me to
promise, so I did.

ETHEL :

Well, that's settled then. (*jumping up*) And
won't it be nice to be *married*. Really *married!*
. . . And now I want to *do* something. I'm
tired of sitting still. What shall it be?

GEOFFREY
(*with brilliant originality*) :

We might go for a walk up Milverton Hill. The
view there's awfully fine. (*looks at watch*) But
there's hardly time before lunch.

ETHEL :

Besides, I should spoil my shoes. (*puts out foot, the shoe of which is manifestly not* intended *for country walking*)

GEOFFREY :

Suppose we go to the strawberry bed and eat strawberries?

ETHEL :

Oh, yes, that'll be splendid. I can be so deliciously greedy over strawberries. (*puts her arm in his, and he leads her off to the strawberry beds. As they go off,* MRS. CASSILIS, LADY MARCHMONT, *and* MRS. BORRIDGE *come out from house)*

MRS. CASSILIS :

Going for a stroll, dears?

GEOFFREY :

Only as far as the strawberry bed, mother dear.

MRS. CASSILIS :

Oughtn't dear Ethel to have a hat? The sun is very hot there.

ETHEL :

I've got a parasol, Mrs. Cassilis.
(*They disappear down the path.*)

MRS. BORRIDGE
(*rallying her*) :

You weren't down to breakfast, Lady Marchmont.

LADY MARCHMONT :

No, I—had a headache.

MRS. CASSILIS :

Poor Margaret.

MRS. BORRIDGE
(*sympathetically*) :

It's 'eadachy weather, isn't it.   (*subsiding into a
chair.   MRS. BORRIDGE makes it a rule of life never
to stand when she can sit*)

LADY MARCHMONT :

I suppose it is.

MRS. BORRIDGE :

Or perhaps it was the oyster patties last night?
I've often noticed after an oyster I come over quite
queer.   Specially if it isn't quite fresh.

LADY MARCHMONT :

Indeed !

MRS. BORRIDGE :

Yes.   But crabs is worse.   Crabs is simply poison
to me.

LADY MARCHMONT

(*faintly*) :

How extràordinary.

MRS. BORRIDGE :

They are, I do assure you.   If I touch a crab I'm
that ill nobody would believe it.

MRS. CASSILIS :

Well, Margaret, I expect you oughtn't to be
talked to or it will make your head worse.   You
stay here quietly and rest while I take Mrs. Borridge for a stroll in the garden.

LADY MARCHMONT:

Thank you.   (closing her eyes)   My head is a little bad still.

MRS. BORRIDGE

(confidentially):

Try a drop of brandy, Lady Marchmont.   My 'usband always said there's nothing like brandy if you're feeling poorly.

LADY MARCHMONT:

Thank you.   I think I'll just try what rest will do.

MRS. CASSILIS

(making LADY MARCHMONT comfortable):

I expect that will be best.   Put your head back, dear.   Headaches are such trying things, aren't they, Mrs. Borridge?   This way.   And you're to keep quite quiet till luncheon, Margaret.   (Exeunt MRS. CASSILIS and MRS. BORRIDGE.   LADY MARCHMONT closes her eyes, with a sigh of relief.   After a moment enter BUTLER from house, with MRS. HERRIES)

BUTLER:

Mrs. Herries.

LADY MARCHMONT

(rises, and goes up to meet her):

How do you do?   Mrs. Cassilis is in the garden, Watson.   (to MRS. HERRIES)   She has just gone for a stroll with Mrs. Borridge.

MRS. HERRIES:

Oh, pray don't disturb her.   Pray don't.   I can only stay for a moment.   Literally a moment.

LADY MARCHMONT:

But she would be so sorry to miss you. Will you let her know, Watson? She went that way. (*pointing to path along which* MRS. CASSILIS *went a moment before*)

BUTLER :

Yes, my lady.

LADY MARCHMONT:

And how's the dear Rector? (*she and* MRS. HERRIES *sit*) You've not brought him with you?

MRS. HERRIES:

No. He was too busy. There is always so much to do in these *small* parishes, isn't there?

LADY MARCHMONT:

Indeed?

MRS. HERRIES:

Oh, yes. There's the garden—and the pigs. The Rector is devoted to his pigs, you know. And his roses.

LADY MARCHMONT:

The Rector's roses are quite famous, aren't they? (*But* MRS. HERRIES *has not come to Deynham to talk horticulture, but to inquire about a far more interesting subject. She looks round cautiously, and then, lowering her voice to an undertone, puts the important question.*)

MRS. HERRIES:

And now tell me, dear Lady Marchmont, before Mrs. Cassilis comes back, what is she like?

LADY MARCHMONT
(*laughing slightly*):

Really, dear Mrs. Herries, I think I must leave you to decide that for yourself.

MRS. HERRIES
(*sighs*):

So bad as that! The Rector feared so. And the mother? (*no answer*) Just so! What a pity. An *orphan* is so much easier to deal with.

LADY MARCHMONT:

You may be glad to hear that Mr. Borridge *is* dead.

MRS. HERRIES:

So Mrs. Cassilis said. How fortunate! How very fortunate! (MRS. CASSILIS, *followed* by MRS. BORRIDGE, return *from their walk*. WATSON *brings up the rear*)

MRS. HERRIES:

Dear Mrs. Cassilis, how do you do? (*sympathetically*) *How* are you?

MRS. CASSILIS
(*rather amused at* MRS. HERRIES'S *elaborate bedside manner*):

Quite well, thanks. It's Margaret who is unwell.

MRS. HERRIES

Indeed! She didn't mention it.

LADY MARCHMONT
(*hurriedly*):

I have a headache.

MRS. HERRIES :

I'm so sorry.

MRS. CASSILIS
(*sweetly*) :

You have heard of my son's engagement, haven't you. Dear Ethel is with us now, I'm glad to say. Let me introduce you to her mother.

MRS. HERRIES :

How do you do? (*bows*) What charming weather we're having, aren't we?

MRS. CASSILIS :

You'll stay to luncheon now you are here, won't you? (MRS. BORRIDGE *subsides into a chair*)

MRS. HERRIES :

I'm afraid I mustn't. I left the Rector at home. He will be expecting me.

MRS. CASSILIS :

Why didn't you bring him with you?

MRS. HERRIES :

So kind of you, dear Mrs. Cassilis. (*nervously*) But he hardly liked—— How is poor Geoffrey?

MRS. CASSILIS
(*cheerfully*) :

He's very well. He's in the kitchen garden with Ethel. At the strawberry bed. You'll see them if you wait.

MRS. HERRIES
(*hastily*) :

I'm afraid I can't. In fact, I must run away at once. I only looked in in passing. It's nearly one o'clock, and the Rector always likes his luncheon at one. (*shakes hands with gush of sympathetic (fervour*) Good-bye, dear Mrs. Cassilis. (*frigidly*) Good-bye, Mrs. Borridge. (*bows*)

MRS. BORRIDGE
(*stretching out her hand*):

Good-bye, Mrs.—I didn't rightly catch your name.

MRS. HERRIES :

Herries. Mrs. Herries. (*shakes hands nervously*)

MRS. BORRIDGE
(*heartily*):

Good-bye, Mrs. 'Erris.

MRS. CASSILIS :

And you're coming over to dine on Thursday? That's to-day week, you know. *And* the Rector, of course. You won't forget?

MRS. HERRIES :

With pleasure. Good-bye, Lady Marchmont. (*looks at* MRS. BORRIDGE, *who has turned away, then at* LADY MARCHMONT, *then goes off, much depressed, into the house. Pause*)

MRS. BORRIDGE :

I think I'll be going in, too, Mrs. Cassilis, just to put myself straight for dinner.

MRS. CASSILIS :

Yes. Do. Luncheon will be ready in half an hour. (MRS. BORRIDGE *waddles off into the house complacently.*   LADY MARCHMONT *sinks limply into a chair, with a smothered groan.*   MRS. CASSILIS *resumes her natural voice*)   How's your headache, Margaret?   Better?

LADY MARCHMONT:

Quite well.   In fact, I never had a headache. That was a little deception on my part, dear, to excuse my absence from the breakfast table.   Will you forgive me?   (MRS. CASSILIS *nods without a smile.   She looks perfectly wretched.* LADY MARCHMONT *makes a resolute effort to cheer her up by adopting a light tone, but it is obviously an effort*) Breakfasts *are* rather a mistake, aren't they?   So trying to the temper.   And that awful woman!   I felt a brute for deserting you.   On the very first morning, too.   But I didn't feel strong enough to face her again so soon.   How *could* Geoffrey do it!

MRS. CASSILIS
(grimly):

Geoffrey's not going to marry *Mrs.* Borridge.

LADY MARCHMONT:

He's going to marry the daughter.   And she'll grow like her mother ultimately.   All girls do, poor things.

MRS. CASSILIS
(sighs):

Poor Geoffrey.   I suppose there's something wrong in the way we bring boys up.   When they reach manhood they seem quite unable to distinguish between the right sort of woman and—the other sort. A pretty face, and they're caught at once. It's only after they've lived for a few years in the world and got soiled and hardened—got what we call experience, in fact—that they even begin to understand the difference.

LADY MARCHMONT
(*decidedly*):

You ought to have sent Geoffrey to a public school. His father ought to have insisted on it.

MRS. CASSILIS:

Poor Charley died when Geoff was only twelve. And when I was left alone I couldn't make up my mind to part with him. Besides, I hate the way public school boys look on women.

LADY MARCHMONT:

Still, it's a safeguard.

MRS. CASSILIS
(*dismally*) ·

Perhaps it is.
(*Neither of the sisters speak for a moment. Both are plunged in painful thought. Suddenly* LADY MARCHMONT *looks up and catches sight of* MRS. CASSILIS'S *face, which looks drawn and miserable. She goes over to her with something like a cry.*)

LADY MARCHMONT:

My dear Adelaide, don't look like that. You frighten me.

MRS. CASSILIS
(*pulling herself together*):

What's the matter?

LADY MARCHMONT :

Your face looked absolutely *grey!* Didn't you sleep last night?

MRS. CASSILIS :

Not very much. (trying to *smile*) Has my hair gone grey, too?

LADY MARCHMONT :

Of course not.

MRS. CASSILIS :

I feared it might.

LADY MARCHMONT :

You poor dear!

MRS. CASSILIS
(*impulsively*) :

I *am* pretty still, am I not, Margaret?

LADY MARCHMONT :

My dear, you look perfectly sweet, as you always do. Only there *are* one or two little lines I hadn't noticed before. But your *hair's* lovely.

MRS. CASSILIS
(*eagerly*) :

I'm glad of that. I shall need all my looks now— for Geoffrey's sake.

LADY MARCHMONT
(*puzzled*) :

Geoffrey's?

MRS. CASSILIS:

Looks mean so much to a man, don't they? And he has always admired me. Now I shall want him to admire me more than ever.

LADY MARCHMONT:

Why, dear?

MRS. CASSILIS
(*with cold* intensity):

Because I have a rival.

LADY MARCHMONT:

This detestable girl?

MRS. CASSILIS
(nods):

Yes.

LADY MARCHMONT:

My dear Adelaide, isn't it too late now?

MRS. CASSILIS:

Too late? Why, the time has scarcely begun. At present Geoffrey is over head and ears in love with her. While that goes on we can do nothing. (*with absolute conviction*) But it won't last.

LADY MARCHMONT
(*surprised at her confidence*):

Won't it?

MRS. CASSILIS:

No. That kind of love never does. It dies because it is a thing of the senses only. It has no foundation in reason, in common tastes, common interests, common associations. So it dies. (*with a bitter smile*) *My* place is by its death bed.

LADY MARCHMONT
(*with a slight shudder*):

That sounds rather ghoulish.

MRS. CASSILIS:

It *is*.

LADY MARCHMONT
(*more lightly*):

Are you going to do anything to hasten its demise?

MRS. CASSILIS
(*quite practical*):

Oh, yes. In the first place, they're to stay here for a long visit. I want them to feel thoroughly at home. Vulgar people are so much more vulgar when they feel at home, aren't they?

LADY MARCHMONT:

You can hardly expect any change in that direction from *Mrs.* Borridge.

MRS. CASSILIS
(*a short, mirthless laugh*):

I suppose not. (*practical again*) Then I shall ask lots of people to meet them. Oh, lots of people. So that Geoffrey may have the benefit of the contrast. I've asked Mabel to stay, by the way—for a week—to help to entertain dear Ethel. When those two are together it should open Geoffrey's eyes more than anything.

LADY MARCHMONT:

Love is blind.

MRS. CASSILIS
(*briskly*) :

It sees a great deal better than it used to do, dear.
Far better than it did when *we* were young people.
(*pause*)

LADY MARCHMONT :

Anything else?

MRS. CASSILIS :

Not at the moment. (*a ghost of a smile*) Yes,
by the way. There's Major Warrington.

LADY MARCHMONT
(*shocked*) :

You're not really going to consult that dissipated
wretch?

MRS. CASSILIS
(*recklessly*) :

I would consult the Witch of Endor if I thought
she could help me—and if I knew her address. Oh,
I'm prepared to go any lengths. I wonder if he
would elope with her for a consideration?

LADY MARCHMONT
(*horrified*) :

Adelaide, you wouldn't do that. It would be
dreadful. Think of the scandal.

MRS. CASSILIS :

My dear, if she would elope with Watson I'd raise
his wages. (*rises*)

LADY MARCHMONT :

Adelaide!

MRS. CASSILIS
(*defiantly*) :

I *would*.   Ah, Margaret, you've no children. (*her voice quivering, and her eyes shining with* intensity *of* emotion)   You don't know how it feels to see your son wrecking his life and not be able to prevent it.   I love my son better than anything else in the whole world.   There is nothing I wouldn't do to save him.   That is how mothers are made. That's what we're for.

LADY MARCHMONT
(*slight shrug*) :

Poor girl !

MRS. CASSILIS
(*fiercely*) :

You're *not* to pity her, Margaret.   I forbid you. She tried to steal away my son.

LADY MARCHMONT :

Still——

MRS. CASSILIS
(*impatiently*) :

Margaret, don't be sentimental.   The girl's not in *love* with Geoffrey.   Anyone can see that.   She's in love with his position and his money, the money he will have some day.   She doesn't really care two straws for him.   It was a trap, a trap from the beginning, and poor Geoff blundered into it.

LADY MARCHMONT :

She couldn't *make* the omnibus horse fall down !

MRS. CASSILIS :

No.   That was chance.   But after that she set herself to catch him, and her mother egged her on no doubt, and taught her how to play her fish.   And you pity her !

LADY MARCHMONT
(*soothingly*) :

I don't really.   At least, I did for a moment.   But I suppose you're right.

MRS. CASSILIS
(*vehemently*) :

Of course I'm right.   I'm Geoffrey's mother. Who should know if I don't?   Mothers have eyes. If she really cared for him I should know.   I might try to blind myself, but I should *know*.   But she doesn't.   And she shan't marry him.   She shan't !

LADY MARCHMONT :

My dear, don't glare at me like that.   *I'm* not trying to make the match.

MRS. CASSILIS :

Was I glaring?

LADY MARCHMONT :

You looked rather tigerish.   (MRS. CASSILIS *gives short laugh.   Pause*) By the way, as she's *not* to be your daughter-in-law, is it necessary to be quite so affectionate to her all the time?   It rather gets on my nerves.

MRS. CASSILIS :

It is absolutely necessary.   If there were any coolness between us the girl would be on her guard,

and Geoffrey would take her side. That would be
fatal. Geoffrey must never know how I feel towards her. No! When this engagement is broken
off I shall kiss her affectionately at parting, and
when the carriage comes round I shall shed tears.

Lady Marchmont
(wondering):

Why?

Mrs. Cassilis:

Because otherwise it would make a division between Geoffrey and me. And I couldn't bear that.
I must keep his love whatever happens. And if I
have to deceive him a little to keep it, isn't that
what we women always have to do? In fact, I
shall have to deceive everybody except you. Lady
Remenham, Mrs. Herries, the whole county. If
they once knew they would be sure to talk. Lady
Remenham never does anything else, does she? And
later on, when the engagement was all over and
done with, Geoffrey would get to hear of it, and
he'd never forgive me.

Lady Marchmont:

My dear, your unscrupulousness appals me.
(Mrs. Cassilis *shrugs impatiently*) Well, it's not
very nice, you must admit.

Mrs. Cassilis
(exasperated):

Nice! Of course it's not *nice*! Good heavens,
Margaret, you don't suppose I *like* doing this sort
of thing, do you? I do it because I must, because
it's the only way to save Geoffrey. If Geoffrey married her, he'd be miserable, and I won't have that.

Of course, it would be *pleasanter* to be perfectly
straightforward, and tell the girl I detest her. But
if I did she'd marry Geoff if only to spite me. So I
must trap her as she has trapped him. It's not a
nice game, but it's the only possible one. (*more
calmly*) Yes, I must be on the best of terms with
Ethel. (*with a smile of real enjoyment at the
thought*) And *you* must make friends with that ap-
palling mother.

LADY MARCHMONT
(*firmly*) :

No, Adelaide! I refuse!

MRS. CASSILIS
(*crosses to her*) :

You must. You *must!* (*takes her two hands
and looks into her eyes*)

LADY MARCHMONT
(*giving way, hypnotised*) :

Very well. I'll do my best. (MRS. CASSILIS
*drops her hands, and turns away with a sigh of
relief*) But I shan't come down to breakfast!
There are limits to my endurance. (*plaintive*) And
I do so hate breakfasting in my room. The crumbs
always get into my bed.

MRS. CASSILIS
(*consoling her*) :

Never mind. When we've won you shall share
the glory.

LADY MARCHMONT
(*doubtfully*) :

You're going to win?

MRS. CASSILIS
(nods):

I'm going to win.   I've no doubt whatever about
that.   I've brains and she hasn't.   And brains
always tell in the end.   Besides, she did something
this morning which made me sure that I should win.

LADY MARCHMONT
(trying *to get back her old lightness of* tone):
She didn't eat with her knife?

MRS. CASSILIS
(*resolutely serious*):

No.   She yawned.

LADY MARCHMONT
(*puzzled*):

Yawned?

MRS. CASSILIS:

Yes.   Three times.   When I saw that I knew
that I should win.

LADY MARCHMONT
(*peevish*):

My dear Adelaide, what *do* you mean?

MRS. CASSILIS:

Girls like that can't endure boredom.   They're
used to excitement, the vulgar excitement of Bohe-
mian life in London.   Theatres, supper parties,
plenty of fast society.   She owned as much this
morning.   Well, down here she shall be dull, oh,
how *dull!*   I will see to that.   The curate shall

come to dinner. And old Lady Bellairs, with her
tracts and her trumpet. I've arranged that it shall
be a long engagement. She shall yawn to some
purpose before it's over. And when she's bored
she'll get cross. You'll see. She'll begin to quarrel with her mother, and nag at Geoffrey—at everyone, in fact, except me. *I* shall be too sweet to her
for that. (*with a long look into her sister's eyes*)
And that will be the beginning of the end.

LADY MARCHMONT
(*turning away her eyes with something like a
shiver*) :

Well, dear, I think your plan diabolical. (*rising*)
But your courage is perfectly splendid, and I love
you for it. (*lays hand on her shoulder for a moment
caressingly*) And now I'll go in and get ready for
lunch.

(LADY MARCHMONT *turns to go into the house. As
she does so the* BUTLER *comes out, followed by*
MABEL *in riding habit.* MRS. CASSILIS'S *manner
changes at once. The intense seriousness with
which she has been talking to her sister disappears
in an instant, and instead you have the charming
hostess, without a care in the world, only thinking
of welcoming her guest and making her comfortable.
It is a triumph of pluck—and breeding.*)

BUTLER :
Lady Mabel Venning.

MRS. CASSILIS
(*rising*) :
Ah, Mabel dear, how are you? (*kisses her*)

You've ridden over?   But you're going to *stay* here,
you know.   Haven't you brought your things?

MABEL :

Mamma is sending them after me.   It was such a
perfect morning for a ride.   How do you do, Lady
Marchmont?   (*shaking hands*)

MRS. CASSILIS.

That's right.   Watson, tell them to take Lady
Mabel's horse round to the stables.   She will keep
it here while she is with us.   (*to* MABEL)   Then
you'll be able to ride every day with Geoffrey.   (to
LADY MARCHMONT)   Poor Ethel doesn't ride.   Isn't
it unfortunate?

LADY MARCHMONT :

Very !

MRS. CASSILIS :

She and Geoffrey are down at the strawberry bed
spoiling their appetites for luncheon.   Would you
like to join them?

MABEL :

I think not, thanks.   It's rather hot, isn't it.   I
think I'd rather stay here with you.

MRS. CASSILIS :

As you please, dear.   (*they sit*)

MABEL :

Oh, before I forget, mamma asked me to tell you
she telegraphed to Uncle Algernon yesterday, and
he's coming down next Wednesday.   She had a

letter from him this morning by the second post. It came just before I started. Such a funny letter. Mamma asked me to bring it to you to read.

Mrs. Cassilis

(*taking letter, and reading it aloud to her sister*): " My dear Julia,—I am at a loss to understand to what I owe the honour of an invitation to Milverton. I thought I had forfeited all claim to it for ever. I can only suppose you have at last found an heiress to marry me. If this is so I may as well say at once that unless she is both extremely rich and extremely pretty I shall decline to entertain her proposal. My experience is that that is a somewhat unusual combination. I will be with you next Wednesday.— Your affectionate brother, A. L. Warrington." (*giving back letter*) That's right, then. And now I think I'll just go down to the kitchen garden and tell Geoffrey you're here. (*rises*) No, don't come too. You stay and entertain Margaret. (*she goes off by the path leading to the strawberry beds*)

Lady Marchmont :

Dear Major Warrington. He always was the most delightfully witty, wicked creature. I'm so glad he's coming while I'm here. Adelaide must be sure and ask him over.

Mabel :

Uncle Algernon is coming over to dine this day week—with mamma.

Lady Marchmont :

To be sure; I remember.
(*Enter* Geoffrey *quickly from garden.*)

GEOFFREY :

Hallo, Mabel. How do you do? (*shaking hands*) I didn't know you were here.

MABEL :

Mrs. Cassilis has just gone to tell you.

GEOFFREY :

I know. She met us as we were coming back from eating strawberries. We've been perfect pigs. She and Ethel will be here in a moment. I ran on ahead.

LADY MARCHMONT
(*rising*) :

Well, it's close on lunch time. I shall go in and get ready.

(LADY MARCHMONT *goes off into the house, leaving the young people together. They begin to chatter at once with the easy familiarity of long acquaintance.*)

GEOFFREY :

You rode over? (*sitting on the arm of her chair*)

MABEL :

Yes, on Basil. He really is the sweetest thing. I like him much better than Hector.

GEOFFREY :

Poor old Hector. He's not so young as he was

MABEL :

No.

(GEOFFREY *suddenly remembers that there is something more important than horses which he has to say before* ETHEL *arrives. He hesitates for a moment, and then plunges into his subject.)*

GEOFFREY :

Mabel. . . . There's something I want to ask you.

MABEL :

Is there?

GEOFFREY :

Yes. But I don't know how to say it. (*hesitates again*)

MABEL
(*smiling*) :

Perhaps you'd better not try, then?

GEOFFREY :

I must. I feel I ought. It's about something Aunt Margaret said yesterday. . . . (*blushing a little*) Mabel, did you ever . . . did I ever . . . did I ever do anything to make you think I . . . I was going to ask you to marry me? (*looking her bravely in the face*)

MABEL
(*turning her eyes away*) :

No, Geoff.

GEOFFREY :

Sure?

MABEL :

Quite sure.

GEOFFREY :

I'm glad.

MABEL
(looking up, surprised):

Why, Geoff?

GEOFFREY:

Because from what Aunt Margaret said I was afraid, without intending it, I'd . . . I—hadn't been quite honourable.

MABEL
(gently):

You have always been everything that is honourable, Geoff. And everything that is kind.

GEOFFREY
(relieved):

Thank you, Mabel. You're a brick, you know. 'And we shall always be friends, shan't we?

MABEL:

Always. (rises)

GEOFFREY:

And you'll be friends with Ethel, too?

MABEL:

If she'll let me.

GEOFFREY:

Of course she'll let you. She's the dearest girl. She's ready to be friends with everybody. And she'll love you, I know. (stands up) You promise? (holds out hand)

MABEL
(takes it):

I promise.
(MRS. CASSILIS and ETHEL enter at this moment

from garden. MRS. CASSILIS *has her arm in* ETHEL'S, *and they make a picture of mutual trust and affection which would make* LADY MARCHMONT *scream. Luckily, she is safely in her room washing her hands.* MRS. CASSILIS *smiles sweetly at* MABEL *as she speaks, but does not relax her hold on her future daughter-in-law.*)

MRS. CASSILIS :

Not gone in to get ready yet, Mabel?

MABEL :

No. Lady Marchmont only went a minute ago.

MRS. CASSILIS
(*to* ETHEL) :

You've not met Mabel yet, have you? I must introduce you. Miss Borridge—Lady Mabel Venning. (*sweetly*) I want you two to be great friends! (*they shake hands*) And now come in and get ready for luncheon. (*they all move towards the house as the curtain falls*)

ACT III.

SCENE :—*The smoking-room at Deynham. A week has elapsed since the last act, and the time is after dinner. The room has two doors, one leading to the hall and the rest of the house, the other communicating with the billiard-room. There is a fireplace on the left, in which a fire burns brightly. A writing table occupies the centre of the stage.*

Further up is a grand piano. By its side a stand with music on it. Obviously a man's room from the substantial writing table, with the cigar box on it, and the leather-covered armchairs. The " Field " and the " Sportsman " lie on a sofa hard by. The room is lighted by lamps. The stage is empty when the curtain rises. Then GEOFFREY *enters from hall. He crosses to the door of the billiard-room, opens it, and looks in. Then turns and speaks to* MAJOR WARRINGTON, *who has just entered from hall.* WARRINGTON *is a cheerful, rather dissipated-looking man of five and forty.*

GEOFFREY :

It's all right, Warrington. They've lighted the lamps.

WARRINGTON :

Good.   (*strolling across towards fireplace*)

GEOFFREY
(*at door of billiard-room*) :
How many will you give me?

WARRINGTON :

Oh, hang billiards.   I'm not up to a game to-night.   That was only an excuse to get away from the women.   I believe that's why games were invented.   But if you *could* get me a whisky and soda I should be your eternal debtor.   Julia kept such an infernally strict watch on me all the evening that I never got more than a glass and a half of champagne.   A fellow can't get along on *that*, can he?

GEOFFREY :

I'll ring.

WARRINGTON :

Do. There's a good fellow. (GEOFFREY *rings*)
Every man requires a certain amount of liquid per
day. I've seen the statistics in the " Lancet." But
Julia never reads the " Lancet." Women never do
read anything, I believe.

GEOFFREY :

Have another cigar?

WARRINGTON :

Thanks. Don't mind if I do. (*takes one and
lights* it) Aren't you going to?

GEOFFREY
(*who looks seedy and out of spirits*) :

No, thanks. (enter FOOTMAN, *with whisky and
soda*) *and glasses on tray*) Whisky and soda, James.

FOOTMAN :

Yes, sir. (*puts it on small table and goes out*)

WARRINGTON :

Off your smoke?

GEOFFREY :

Yes. (*pouring whisky*) Say when.

WARRINGTON :

When. (*takes soda*) You're not going to have
one?

GEOFFREY :

No.

WARRINGTON :

Off your drink?

GEOFFREY :

Yes.

WARRINGTON :

That's bad. What's the matter? (*selects comfortable easy chair and sits lazily*)

GEOFFREY :

Oh, nothing. I'm a bit out of sorts, I suppose.

WARRINGTON :

How well your mother looks to-night, by the way! Jove, what a pretty woman she is!

GEOFFREY :

Dear mother.

WARRINGTON
(*sips whisky meditatively*) :

How does she like this marriage of your's?

GEOFFREY
(*off-hand*) :

All right.

WARRINGTON :

Ah. (*nods*)   Bites on the bullet.   No offence, my dear fellow.   I like her pluck.

GEOFFREY
(*exasperated*) :

I assure you, you're mistaken. My mother's been kindness itself over my engagement. She's never said a word against it from the first. I believe she's the only person in this infernal county who hasn't.

WARRINGTON :

Except myself.

GEOFFREY :

Except yourself. And *you* think me a thundering young fool.

WARRINGTON :

Oh, no.

GEOFFREY :

Oh, yes. I could see you looking curiously at me all through dinner—when you weren't eating—as if I were some strange beast. You think I'm a fool, right enough.

WARRINGTON

(*stretching himself luxuriously*) :

Not at all. Miss Borridge is a very pretty girl, very bright, very amusin'. I sat next her at dinner, you know. Not quite the sort one *marries*, perhaps —as a rule——

GEOFFREY

(*crossly*) :

What do you mean?

WARRINGTON

(*shrugs*) :

Anyhow, you're going to marry her. So much the better for *her*. What amuses me is your bringing her old reprobate of a mother down here. The cheek of it quite takes away my breath.

GEOFFREY

(*peevish*) :

What's the matter with her mother? She's common, of course, and over-eats herself, but lots of people do that. And she's good-natured. That's more than some women are.

WARRINGTON
(looking *thoughtfully at the end of his* cigar):

Still, she's scarcely the sort one introduces to one's *mother*, eh? But I'm old-fashioned, no doubt. There's no saying what you young fellows will do. Your code is peculiarly your own. (*wanders across in quest of another whisky and soda*)

GEOFFREY
(restively):

Look here, Warrington, what do you mean?

WARRINGTON
(easily):

Want to hit me in the eye, don't you? *I* know. Very natural feeling. Lots of people have it.

GEOFFREY
(sulkily):

Why shouldn't I introduce her to my mother?

WARRINGTON:

Well, she's a disreputable old woman, you know. She lived with Borridge for years before he married her. The other daughter's—— (*shrugs shoulders*) And then to bring her down here and introduce her to Julia! Gad, I like your humour.

GEOFFREY
(*much perturbed at his companion's news*):

Are **you** sure?

WARRINGTON
(nonchalantly):

Sure? Why, it's common knowledge. Everybody knows old Borridge, and most people loathe her. I don't. I rather like her in a way. She's so splendidly vulgar. Flings her aitches about with reckless indifference. And I like her affection for that girl. She's really fond of *her*. So much the worse for you, by the way. You'll never be able to keep them apart.

GEOFFREY
(*irritably*):

Why should I want to keep them apart?

WARRINGTON:

Why should you——? (drinks) Oh, well, my dear chap, if you're satisfied——

GEOFFREY
(*low voice*):

Her sister . . .? Poor Ethel! Poor Ethel!

WARRINGTON
(*with a good-natured effort to make the best of things*):

My dear chap, don't be so down in the mouth. There's no use fretting. I'd no idea you were so completely in the dark about all this, or I wouldn't have told you. Cheer up.

GEOFFREY
(*huskily*):

I'm glad you told me.

WARRINGTON :

To think you've been engaged all this time and never found it out.   What amazing innocence! (*chuckling*) Ha! Ha! . . Ha! Ha! Ha!

GEOFFREY :

Don't. (*sinks on to sofa with a groan*)

WARRINGTON :

Sorry, my dear boy. But it's so devilish amusing.

GEOFFREY :

How blind I've been !   How utterly blind !

WARRINGTON
(*shrugs shoulders*) :

Well, I rather like a chap who's a bit of an ass myself.

GEOFFREY :

Poor mother !

WARRINGTON :

Doesn't she know?   Not about old Borridge? (GEOFFREY *shakes his head*) She must !   Women always do.   They have an instinct about these things that is simply uncanny.   It's often highly inconvenient, too, by the way. She probably says nothing on your account.

GEOFFREY
(*dismally*) :

Perhaps so.   Or Ethel's.   She's been wonderfully kind to Ethel ever since she came down.   Perhaps that's the reason. (*rises*)   After all, it's not Ethel's fault.

WARRINGTON :

Of course not. (*looks at him curiously, then, with an* instinct *of kindliness, goes to him and lays hand on shoulder*) Well, here's luck, my dear boy, and I won't say may you never repent it, but may you put off repenting it as long as possible. That's the best one can hope of most marriages.

GEOFFREY
(*drily*) :

Thanks !

WARRINGTON :

Well, it's been an uncommon amusin' evening. Mrs. Herries' face has been a study for a lifetime. And as for Julia's—oh, outraged respectability ! What a joy it is !
(*Further conversation is interrupted by the entrance of the other guests from the hall. These are* LADY REMENHAM, LADY MARCHMONT, MRS. HERRIES, MRS. BORRIDGE, ETHEL, *and* MABEL. *Last of all comes the* RECTOR, *with* MRS. CASSILIS. They enter with *a hum of conversation.*)

RECTOR
(*to his hostess*) :

Well, he's a disreputable poaching fellow. It's no more than he deserved.

MRS. CASSILIS
(nods dubiously) :

Still, I'm sorry for his wife.

MRS. HERRIES :

I'll send down to her in the morning and see if she wants anything.

MRS. BORRIDGE·

(*beaming with good humour*):
So this is where you gentlemen have got to!

GEOFFREY :

I brought Major Warrington to smoke a cigar.

LADY REMENHAM

(*looking fixedly at whisky then at* WARRINGTON):
Algernon!

WARRINGTON
(*protesting*):

My dear Julia, I believe there is nothing unusual
in a man's requiring *one* whisky and soda at this
time in the evening.

LADY REMENHAM :

I trust it has been only one. (*sits on sofa, where
she is joined by* LADY MARCHMONT)

WARRINGTON

(*changing the subject*):

Whom have you been sending to jail for poaching now, Rector? No Justice's justice, I hope?

RECTOR :

Old Murcatt. He's one of Mrs. Cassilis's ten-
ants. A most unsatisfactory fellow. He was
caught red-handed laying a snare in the Milverton
woods. It was a clear case. (ETHEL *stifles a yawn*)

ETHEL :

I should have thought there was no great harm
in that.

RECTOR :

My dear young lady !

MRS. CASSILIS :

Take care, Ethel dear. An Englishman's hares are sacred.

MRS. BORRIDGE :

How silly ! I can't bear 'are myself. (*seats herself massively in armchair in front of piano. An awkward silence follows this insult to hares. As it threatens to grow oppressive, the* RECTOR *tries what can be done with partridges to bridge the gulf)*

RECTOR :

You'll have plenty of partridges this year, Mrs. Cassilis. We started five coveys as we drove here.

MRS. CASSILIS
(*acknowledging his help with a smile*) :

We generally have a good many. (ETHEL, *stifling another yawn, strolls to piano, opens it, and strikes a note or two idly*)

MABEL :

You play, I know, Ethel. Won't you play something?

ETHEL
(*sulkily*) :

No. (*turns away, closing piano sharply. Another constrained silence)*

RECTOR :

I saw you out riding to-day, Mabel. I looked in at Dobson's cottage. Poor fellow, I'm afraid he's very ill.

MABEL:

Yes. I was with Geoffrey. We had a long ride, all through Lower Milverton and Carbury to Mirstoke. It was delightful.

MRS. BORRIDGE
(to MRS. HERRIES):

Your husband has a lot of that sort of thing to do down here, I suppose, Mrs. 'Erris?

MRS. HERRIES
(with frosty politeness):

When people are ill they generally like a visit from a clergyman, don't they?

MRS. BORRIDGE
(bluntly):

Well, there's no accounting for tastes. My 'usband, when he was ill, wouldn't 'ave a parson near 'im. Said it gave 'im the creeps.
(Another silence that can be felt. WARRINGTON'S shoulders quiver with delight, and he chokes hurriedly into a newspaper.)

LADY MARCHMONT
(crossing to fire, with polite pretence that it is the physical, not the social, atmosphere that is freezing her to the bone):

How sensible of you to have a fire, Adelaide.

MRS. CASSILIS
(throwing her a grateful look):

It is pleasant, isn't it? These August evenings are often cold in the country.
(ETHEL stifles a prodigious yawn.)

GEOFFREY
(going to her):

Tired, Ethel?

ETHEL
(pettishly):

No. *(glowers at him. He turns away with slight shrug. There is yet another awkward pause)*

MRS. CASSILIS
(rising nervously):

Won't somebody play billiards? Are the lamps lighted, Geoffrey?

GEOFFREY:

Yes, mother.

MRS. CASSILIS:

Or shall we play pyramids? Then we can all join in. *(persuasively)* You'll play, Mrs. Borridge, I'm sure?

MRS. BORRIDGE
(beaming):

I'm on.

MRS. CASSILIS:

You, Lady Remenham?

LADY REMENHAM:

No, thanks. Mrs. Herries and I are going to stay by the fire and talk about the Rector's last sermon. *(the RECTOR raises hands in horror)*

MRS. CASSILIS:

Margaret?

Lady Marchmont :

No, really.   I've never played pyramids in my life.

Mrs. Borridge

(in *high good humour*)

Then it's 'igh time you began, Lady Marchmont. *I'll* teach you.

(Mrs. Cassilis *looks* entreaty.   Lady Marchmont *assents, smiling.*)

Lady Marchmont :

Very well.   To please you, dear Mrs. Borridge! (Lady Marchmont *goes off* to *billiard-room, fol*-lowed *a moment later* by Mabel)

Mrs. Cassilis :

You, Mabel?   That's three.   Ethel four.

Ethel :

No, thank you, Mrs. Cassilis.   I won't play.

Mrs. Borridge :

Why not, Eth?   You're a nailer at pyramids.

Ethel
(*pettishly*) :

Because I'd rather not, mother.   (*turns away*)

Mrs. Borridge :

All right, dearie.   You needn't snap my nose off. [*goes off* to *billiard-room with unruffled cheerfulness*)

MRS. CASSILIS:

Geoffrey five. The Rector six.

RECTOR:

Very well, if you won't play for money. I've no conscientious objections to playing for money, but whenever I do it I always lose. Which comes to the same thing. (*follows* MRS. BORRIDGE *off*)

MRS. CASSILIS:

You, Major Warrington, of course?

WARRINGTON
(*laughing*):

No, thanks. I shall stay here and flirt with Mrs. Herries.

MRS. CASSILIS:

Very well. How many did I say? Six, wasn't it? And myself seven. Coming, Geoff?

GEOFFREY:

All right, mother. (GEOFFREY *looks doubtfully at* ETHEL *for a moment, and even takes a step towards her, but she takes no notice of him. Baffled, he turns to his mother, who leads him off after the others.* LADY REMENHAM *settles herself comfortably in armchair above the fireplace.* MRS. HERRIES *takes another by her, and they begin to gossip contentedly.* ETHEL *looks sullenly in their direction.* WARRINGTON *makes a valiant effort to retrieve his glass from the mantelpiece, with a view to replenishing it with whisky*)

LADY REMENHAM :

Now, Mrs. Herries, draw up that chair to the fire,
and we'll talk scandal.

WARRINGTON

(*stretching out hand towards glass*) :

The Rector's sermon, Julia !

LADY REMENHAM :

Algernon ! (*he stops dead*)
(ETHEL *seats herself in the armchair behind the
writing table, puts her elbows on the table, and
glares into vacancy, looking rather like a handsome
fury. Presently* WARRINGTON *joins her. She yawns
with unaffected weariness.* WARRINGTON *looks at
her with an amused smile.*)

WARRINGTON :

Bored, Miss Borridge?

ETHEL :

I wonder.

WARRINGTON

(*draws up chair by her*) :

I don't. (*she laughs*) Life isn't very lively down
here till the shooting begins.

ETHEL

(*drumming with her fingers on table*) :

I don't shoot. So I'm afraid that won't help me
much.

WARRINGTON :

I remember.   Nor ride, I think you told me?

ETHEL
(yawns) :

Nor ride.

WARRINGTON :

Gad.   I'm sorry for you.

ETHEL
(looking curiously at him) :

I believe you really are.

WARRINGTON :

Of course I am.

ETHEL :

I don't know about " of course."   Except for
Mrs. Cassilis—and poor Geoff—who doesn't count—
I don't find much sympathy in this part of the coun-
try.   Heigho!   How they hate me!

WARRINGTON
(protesting) :

No.   No.

ETHEL :

Oh, yes, they do.   Every one of them.   From
Watson, who pours out my claret at dinner, and
would dearly love to poison it, to your sister, who is
glaring at us at this moment.

(As, indeed, LADY REMENHAM is doing with some
intensity.   She highly disapproves of her brother's
attentions to ETHEL, but, as there is no very obvious

method of stopping them, she says nothing. Presently she and MRS. HERRIES *begin a game of bezique, and that, for the time at least, distracts her attention from her brother's depravity.*)

WARRINGTON

(*looking up and laughing*):

Dear Julia. She never had any manners.

ETHEL:

She's no worse than the rest. Mrs. Herries would do just the same if she dared. And as for Mabel—— !

WARRINGTON:

Don't hit it off with Mabel?

ETHEL:

Oh, we don't quarrel, if that's what you mean, or call one another names across the table. I wish we did. I could beat her at that. We're as civil as the Devil. (*he laughs*) What *are* you laughing at?

WARRINGTON:

Only at the picturesqueness of your language.

ETHEL
(*shrugs*):

Yes, Mabel despises me, and I *hate* her.

WARRINGTON:

Why?

ETHEL
(*wearily*):

Because we're different, I suppose. She's everything I'm not. She's well-born and well-bred. Her father's an earl. Mine was a bookmaker.

WARRINGTON :

Is that all?

ETHEL
(bitterly) :

No. She's running after Geoffrey. (WARRING-TON looks incredulous) She is!

WARRINGTON
(raising eyebrows) :

Jealous?

ETHEL :

Yes. I am jealous. Little beast! (picks up flimsy paper knife) I'd like to kill her. (makes savage jab with knife. It promptly breaks)

WARRINGTON
(taking pieces out of her hand) :

Don't be violent. (carries pieces blandly to fire. ETHEL stares straight in front of her. Meantime LADY REMENHAM has been conversing in an under-tone with MRS. HERRIES, occasionally glancing over her shoulder at the other two. In the sudden hush which follows WARRINGTON'S movement to-wards the fireplace her voice suddenly becomes alarmingly audible)

LADY REMENHAM :

Such a common little thing, too! And I don't even call her pretty.

MRS. HERRIES :

It's curious how Mrs. Cassilis seems to have taken
to her.

LADY REMENHAM :

Yes. She even tolerates that awful mother.
(irritably) What *is* it, Algernon?

WARRINGTON
(*blandly*) :

Only a little accident with a paper knife. (LADY
REMENHAM *grunts.* WARRINGTON *returns to* ETHEL)

MRS. HERRIES
(lowering *her* voice discreetly) :

For Geoffrey's sake, of course. She's so devoted
to him.

LADY REMENHAM :

It may be that. *I'm* inclined to think her mind
has given way a little. I asked her about it last
week. (*the two ladies drop their voices again to a
murmur, but* ETHEL *has heard the last remark or
two, and* looks *like murder*)

WARRINGTON
(*sitting by* ETHEL, *and resuming interrupted
thread*) :

You were going to tell me what makes you think
Mabel is in love with Geoffrey.

ETHEL :

Was I?

WARRINGTON :

Weren't you?

ETHEL :

Well, perhaps I will.

WARRINGTON :

Go ahead.

ETHEL :

She's staying here, and they're always together. They ride almost every morning. I can't ride, you know. And Geoffrey loves it.

WARRINGTON :

You should take to it.

ETHEL :

I did try one day. They were just starting when I suddenly said I'd like to go with them.

WARRINGTON
(*starting*) :

What did they say to that?

ETHEL :

Oh, Mabel pretended to be as pleased as possible. She lent me an old habit, and Geoff said they'd let me have a horse that was as quiet as a lamb. Horrid kicking beast !

WARRINGTON :

What horse was it?

ETHEL :

It was called Jasmine, or some such name.

WARRINGTON :

Mrs. Cassilis's mare? Why, my dear girl, she hasn't a kick in her.

ETHEL :

Hasn't she! . . . Anyhow, we started.   So
long as we walked it was all right, and I began to
think I might actually get to like it.   But soon we
began to trot—and that was *awful*.   I simply
screamed.   The beast stopped at once.   But I went
on screaming till they got me off.

WARRINGTON :

What did Geoffrey say?

ETHEL :

Nothing.   But he looked terrible.   Oh, how he
despised me!

WARRINGTON :

Poor girl.

ETHEL :

They brought me back, walking all the way.   And
Geoff offered to give up riding in the mornings if I
liked.   (WARRINGTON *whistles*)   But, of course, I
had to say no.   So now they go out together every
day, and often don't come back till lunch.

WARRINGTON :

And what do *you* do?

ETHEL
(*wearily*) :

I sit at home and yawn and yawn. (*does so*) Mrs.
Cassilis takes me out driving sometimes.   She does
what she can to amuse me.   But of course she's busy
in the mornings.

WARRINGTON :

What does Mrs. Borridge do?

ETHEL :

Lady Marchmont looks after her. I believe she gets a kind of pleasure in leading her on and watching her make a fool of herself. Old cat! And mother sees nothing. She's as pleased with herself as possible. She's actually made Lady Marchmont promise to come and stay with us in London!

WARRINGTON :

Bravo Mrs. Borridge!

ETHEL :

So I sit here in the drawing-room with a book or the newspaper and I'm bored! bored!

WARRINGTON :

And Geoffrey?

ETHEL :

He doesn't seem to notice. If I say anything to him about it he just says I'm not *well!* He's very kind and tries to find things to amuse me, but it's a strain. And so it goes on day after day. Heigho! (*a short silence*)

WARRINGTON :

Well, my dear, I admire your courage.

ETHEL
(*surprised*) :

What do you mean?

WARRINGTON :

A lifetime of this! Year in year out. Till you can yawn yourself decently into your grave.

ETHEL
(*alarmed*):

But it won't always be like this. We sha'n't live here, Geoff and I.

WARRINGTON:

Oh, yes, you will. Mrs. Cassilis was talking only at dinner of the little house she was going to furnish for you both down here, just on the edge of the Park. So that you could always be near her.

ETHEL:

But Geoff has his profession.

WARRINGTON:

His profession is only a name. He makes nothing at it. And never will. Geoffrey's profession is to be a country gentleman and shoot pheasants.

ETHEL:

But we shall have a house in London as well.

WARRINGTON
(*shaking his head*):

Not you. As long as his mother lives Geoffrey will be dependent on her, you know. He has nothing worth calling an income of his own. And he's proud. He won't accept more from her than he's obliged even if her trustees would allow her to hand over anything substantial to him on his marriage—which they wouldn't.

ETHEL
(*defiantly*):

I shall refuse to live down here.

WARRINGTON :

My dear, you won't be asked. You'll have to live where Mrs. Cassilis provides a house for you. Besides, Geoff will prefer it. He likes the country, and he's devoted to his mother.

ETHEL :

Phew !

WARRINGTON :

Happily, it won't last for ever. I dare say you'll have killed poor Mrs. Cassilis off in a dozen years or so. Though you never know how long people will last nowadays, by the way. These modern doctors are the devil.

ETHEL :

Kill her off? What do you mean? I don't want to kill Mrs. Cassilis. I like her.

WARRINGTON
(looking at her in genuine astonishment) :

My dear young lady, you don't suppose you'll be able to stand this sort of thing, do you? Oh, no. You'll kick over the traces, and there'll be no end of a scandal, and Geoff'll blow his brains out—if he's got any—and she'll break her heart, and that'll be the end of it.

ETHEL
(fiercely) :

It won't.

WARRINGTON :

Oh, yes, it will. You don't know what Country Society is. The dulness of it ! How it eats into your bones. *I* do.

ETHEL :

Does it bore *you*, too?

WARRINGTON :

Bore?   It bores me to *tears!*   I'm not a bad lot,
really.   At least, no worse than most middle-aged
bachelors.   But Julia thinks me an utterly abandoned
character, and I take care not to undeceive her.
Why?   Because I find Milverton so intolerable.   I
used to come down every Christmas.   One of those
ghastly family reunions.   A sort of wake without the
corpse.   At last I couldn't stand it, and did something perfectly outrageous.   I forget what.   But I
know the servants all gave warning.   So now I'm
supposed to be thoroughly disreputable, and that
ass Remenham won't have me asked to the house.
Thank Heaven for that.

ETHEL :

But Geoff likes the country.

WARRINGTON :

I dare say.   But Geoffrey and I are different.   So
are Geoffrey and you.   You and I are town birds.
He's a country bumpkin.   *I* know the breed !

ETHEL
(*in* horror) :

And I shall have to stand this all my life ! All my
life ! (*savagely*) I won't ! I won't !

WARRINGTON
(*calmly*) :

You will !

Ethel ::

I won't, I tell you! (Warrington *shrugs*) It's too sickening. (*pause. She seems to think for a moment, then grasps him by the arm, and speaks eagerly, dropping her voice, and looking cautiously over towards the others*) I say, let's go off to Paris, you and I, and leave all this. It'd be awful fun.

Warrington
(*appalled, rising*):

Hush! Hush! For God's sake. Julia'll hear.

Ethel
(*almost in a whisper*):

Never mind. What does it matter? Let's go. You'd enjoy it like anything. We'd have no end of a good time.

Warrington
(*shaking himself free desperately*):

My dear young lady, haven't I just told you that I'm not that sort at all? I'm a perfectly respectable person, of rather austere morality than otherwise.

Ethel

Rot! You'll come? (*grasping his arm again*)

Warrington :

No, I won't. I decline. I can't go off with the girl my host is going to marry. It wouldn't be decent. Besides, I don't want to go off with anybody.

ETHEL

(*her spirits dropping to zero*):

You won't?

WARRINGTON

(testily):

No, I won't.   And, for goodness' sake, speak lower.   Julia's listening with all her ears.

ETHEL:

(*with a* bitter *little laugh*):

Poor Major Warrington! How I scared you!

WARRINGTON:

I should say you did.   I'm not so young as I was. A few years ago, a little thing like that never made me turn a hair.   Now I can't stand it. (*subsiding into chair, and wiping the perspiration from his brow*)

ETHEL:

You've gone through it before, then?

WARRINGTON:

More than once, my dear.

ETHEL

(*dismally*):

And now you'll look down on me, too.

WARRINGTON

(*trying to cheer her up*):

On the contrary, I admire you immensely.   In fact, I don't know which I admire more, your pluck or your truly marvellous self-control. To ask me to go off with you without letting Julia hear! (*looking anxiously towards her*) It was masterly.

ETHEL
(*sighs*):

Well, I suppose I shall have to marry Geoff after all.

WARRINGTON:

I suppose so. Unless you could go off with the Rector? (*she laughs shrilly. The two ladies turn sharply and glare*)

ETHEL:

Now I've shocked your sister again.

WARRINGTON:

You have. She thinks I'm flirting with you. That means I shan't be asked down to Milverton for another five years. Thank heaven for that! Ah, here are the billiard players. (*he rises, with a sigh of relief. The conversation has been amusing, but not without its perils, and he is not altogether sorry to have it safely over. ETHEL remains seated, and does not turn round. The billiard players troop in, headed by* MABEL, GEOFFREY *holding open the door for them*)

GEOFFREY
(*to* MABEL):

You fluked outrageously, you know.

MABEL
(*entering*):

I didn't!

GEOFFREY :

Oh, yes, you did.   Didn't she, mother?

MRS. CASSILIS
(*smiling at her*) :

Disgracefully.

MRS. BORRIDGE :

You'll soon learn, Lady Marchmont, if you prae-
tice a bit.

LADY MARCHMONT :

Do you think so?

LADY REMENHAM :

Well, who won, Rector?

MRS. BORRIDGE :

I did !

LADY REMENHAM :

Indeed? (*turns frigidly away, losing all interest
at once*)

MRS. BORRIDGE
(*obstinately cheerful and friendly*) :

Why didn't *you* play, Mrs. 'Erris?

MRS. HERRIES
(*frigid smile*) :

I never play games.

MRS. BORRIDGE :

You should learn.   I'd teach you.

Mrs. Herries
(*who longs to be as rude as* Lady Remenham *but has not quite the courage*):
Thank you. I fear I have no time. (*joins* Lady Remenham *again, ruffling her feathers nervously*)

Mrs. Cassilis:
Ethel, dear, we missed *you* sadly. I hope you haven't been dull?

Ethel
(*with hysterical laugh*):
Not at all. Major Warrington has been entertaining me.

Rector:
I suspect Miss Borridge felt there would be no opponent worthy of her steel. (Ethel *shrugs her shoulders rudely. He turns away*)

Mrs. Cassilis
(*as a last resort*):
I wonder if we could have some music now. Mabel, dear, won't you sing to us?

Mabel :
I've got nothing with me.

Geoffrey:
Do sing, Mabel. There'll be lots of things you know here. (*opens the piano*) Let me find something. Schumann?

MABEL
(*shakes head*) :

I think not.   (*joins him in searching music stand*)

MRS. CASSILIS :

Sing us that Schubert song you sang when we were dining with you last, dear.

MABEL :

Very well.   Where's Schubert, Geoffrey?

ETHEL
(*to* WARRINGTON) :

Do you see that?   (*watching* GEOFFREY'S *and* MABEL'S *heads in close proximity.   Seems as if she were about to jump from her chair.* WARRINGTON *restrains her by a hand on her arm*)

WARRINGTON :

Sh!   Be quiet, for heaven's sake.

ETHEL
(*hisses*) :

The little *cat!*

MABEL :

Here it is.   Geoff, don't be silly.   (*turns to piano*)

MRS. CASSILIS :

Can you see there?

MABEL :

Yes, thank you.   (*she sings two verses of Schubert's " Adieu," in German, very simply, in a small but sweet voice.   While she sings the behaviour of the guests affords a striking illustration of the English attitude towards music after dinner.* GEOFFREY

stands by piano prepared to turn over when required.
LADY REMENHAM *sits on sofa in an attitude of
seraphic appreciation of her daughter's efforts.*
LADY MARCHMONT, *by her side, is equally enthralled
—and thinks of something else.* MRS. HERRIES
gently beats time with her fan. MRS. CASSILIS *is
sweetly appreciative. The* BORRIDGES, *on the contrary, fall sadly below the standard of polite attention required of them.* ETHEL, *who has begun by
glaring defiantly at* MABEL *during the first few bars
of the song, rapidly comes to the conclusion that she
can't sing, and decides to ignore the whole perform-
ance.* MRS. BORRIDGE *begins by settling herself
placidly to the task of listening. She is obviously
puzzled and rather annoyed when the song turns out
to be German, but decides to put up with it with a
shrug, hoping it will soon be over. At the end of
the first verse she turns to* MRS. CASSILIS *to begin
to talk, but that lady, with a smile and a gesture,
silences her, and the second verse begins. At this*
MRS. BORRIDGE'S *jaw falls, and, after a few bars,
she frankly addresses herself to slumber. Her
purple, good-natured countenance droops upon her
shoulder as the verse proceeds, and when she wakes
up at the end it is with a visible start.* WARRINGTON,
*meantime, has disgraced himself in the eyes of his
sister by talking to* ETHEL *during the opening bars
of the second verse, and has only been reduced to
silence by the stony glare which she thenceforward
keeps fixed upon him till the last bar. In self-
defence, he leans back in his chair and contem-
plates the ceiling resolutely)*

GEOFFREY
(clapping) :

Bravo ! Bravo !

RECTOR :

Charming, charming.

LADY MARCHMONT
(*to* LADY REMENHAM) :

What a sweet voice she has.

MRS. CASSILIS :

Thank you, dear.

RECTOR
(*to* MABEL, *heartily*) :

Now we must have another.

GEOFFREY :

Do, Mabel.

MABEL :

No. That's quite enough.

RECTOR
(*with resolute friendliness*) :

Miss Borridge, *you* sing I'm sure?

MRS. BORRIDGE :

Do, dearie. (*to* LADY REMENHAM) My girl has a
wonderful voice, Lady Remling. Quite like a pro-
fessional. Old Jenkins at the Tiv. used to say she'd
make a fortune in the 'alls.

LADY REMENHAM
(*frigidly*) :

Indeed?

ETHEL :

I don't think I've any songs anyone here would care for.

MRS. BORRIDGE :

Nonsense, dearie. You've lots of songs. Give them " The Children's 'Ome."

ETHEL
(rising) :

Well, I'll sing if you like.

GEOFFREY
(going to her) :

Shall I find you something, Ethel?

ETHEL
(snaps) :

No !

(GEOFFREY turns away snubbed, and joins MABEL. ETHEL goes to the piano, where she is followed a moment later by WARRINGTON, who stands behind it, facing audience, and looking much amused as her song proceeds. ETHEL takes her seat at piano. There is a moment's pause while she darts a glance at GEOFFREY standing with MABEL. Then she seems to make up her mind, and, without prelude of any kind, plunges into the following refined ditty :—

When Joey takes me for a walk, me an' my sister
    Lue,
'E puts 'is arms round both our waists, as lots o'
    men will do.
We don't allow no liberties, and so we tells 'im
    plain,
And Joey says 'e's sorry—but 'e does the same
    again !

(*Spok*en)   Well, we're not going to have that, you know.   Not likely!   We're not that sort.   So we just says to 'im :—

> Stop that, Joey!   Stow it, Joe!
> Stop that ticklin' when I tell yer toe.
> You're too free to suit a girl like me,
> Just you stop that ticklin' or I'll slap yer.

When Joe an' me is man an 'wife—I thinks 'e loves
    me true,
I 'ope 'e'll go on ticklin' me—and leave off ticklin'
    Lue.
'E'll have to leave the girls alone, and mind what
    'e's about,
Or 'im an' me an' Lucy 'ill precious soon fall out.

(*Spok*en)   Yes, I'm not going to put up with that sort of thing once we're married.   Not I.   If 'e tries it on I shall just sing out straight :—

Now then, all of you. (*looks across impudently towards* LADY REMENHAM, *who bristles with indignation*)

> Stop that, Joey!   Chuck it, Joe!
> Stop that ticklin' when I tell yer toe!
> You're too free to suit a girl like me,
> Just you drop that ticklin' or I'll slap yer!

Sings chorus fortissimo, joined by her delighted mother and by WARRINGTON, *who beats time sonorously on the top of the piano.   For this attention she slaps him cordially on the cheek at the last line, by way of giving an artistic finish to the situation, and then rises, flushed and excited, and stands by the piano, looking defiantly at her horrified audience.*

WARRINGTON :

Splendid, by Jove! Capital!

(*That, however, is clearly not the opinion of the rest of the listeners, for the song has what is called a " mixed " reception. The ladies, for the most part, had originally settled themselves into their places prepared to listen to anything which was set before them with polite indifference. A few bars, however, suffice to convince them of the impossibility of that attitude. LADY REMENHAM, who is sitting on the sofa by LADY MARCHMONT, exchanges a horrified glance with that lady, and with MRS. HERRIES on the other side of the room. MABEL looks uncomfortable. The RECTOR feigns abstraction. MRS. CASSILIS remains calm and sweet, but avoids everyone's eye, and more particularly GEOFFREY'S, who looks intensely miserable. But WARRINGTON enjoys himself thoroughly, even down to the final slap, and as for MRS. BORRIDGE, her satisfaction is unmeasured. She beats time to the final chorus, wagging her old head and joining in in stentorian accents, finally jumping up from her chair, clapping her hands, and crying, " That's right, Eth. Give 'em another." In fact, she feels that the song has been a complete triumph for her daughter, and a startling vindication of old Jenkins's good opinion of her powers. Suddenly, however, she becomes conscious of the horrified silence which surrounds her. The cheers die away on her lips. She looks round the room, dazed and almost frightened, then hurriedly reseats herself in her chair, from which she has risen in her excitement, straightens her wig, and—there is an awful pause.*)

Mrs. Cassilis

(feeling she must say something) :
Won't you come to the fire, Ethel? You must be cold out there.

Ethel :

Thank you, Mrs. Cassilis. I'm not cold.

Warrington :

Jove, Miss Borridge, I'd no idea you could sing like that.

Ethel
(with a sneer) :
Nor had Geoffrey.

Lady Remenham
(rising) :
Well, we must be getting home. Geoffrey, will you ask if the carriage is round?

Geoffrey :

Certainly, Lady Remenham. *(rings)*

Mrs. Herries :

We must be going, too. Come, Hildebrand. *(rising also)*

Lady Remenham :

Are you coming with us, Mabel?

Mrs. Cassilis :

Oh, no, I can't spare Mabel yet. She has promised to stay a few days more.

Lady Remenham :

Very well. *(enter Butler)*

GEOFFREY :

Lady Remenham's carriage.

BUTLER :

It's at the door, sir.

GEOFFREY :

Very well. (exit BUTLER)

LADY REMENHAM :

Good-bye, then, dear.   Such a pleasant evening.
Good night, Mabel.   We shall expect you when we
see you.   (general leave takings)

MRS. HERRIES :

Good-bye, Mrs. Cassilis.

MRS. BORRIDGE :

Good night, Lady Remling.   (holds out hand
with nervous cordiality)

LADY REMENHAM :

Good night.   (sweeps past her with icy bow.
MRS. BORRIDGE retires crushed to a chair by fire,
and consoles herself with illustrated paper)

LADY REMENHAM

(to WARRINGTON, who is devoting his last moments
to MISS BORRIDGE) :

Algernon.

WARRINGTON :

Coming, Julia. (to ETHEL) See you in London,
then?

GEOFFREY
(*stiffly*) :

You'll take another cigar, Warrington—to light you home?

WARRINGTON :

Thanks.   Don't mind if I do.   (GEOFFREY *hands box*)

LADY REMENHAM
(*sternly*) :

Algernon.   We're going to get on our wraps. (MRS. CASSILIS *and* LADY REMENHAM, MRS. HERRIES *and the* RECTOR, *go out*)

WARRINGTON :

All right, Julia.   I shall be ready as soon as you are.

GEOFFRE*i*
(*motioning to whisky*) :

Help yourself, Warrington.   (*goes out after the others*)

WARRINGTON
(*to* ETHEL, *after helping himself to drink*) :
Well, my dear, I'm afraid you've done it this time!

ETHEL :

Done what?

WARRINGTON :

Shocked them to some purpose!   It was magnificent, but it was scarcely tactics, eh?

ETHEL :

I suppose not.   (*fiercely*) But I *wanted* to shock them!   Here have they been despising me all the evening for nothing, and when that detestable girl with a voice like a white mouse sang her German jargon, praising her sky-high. I said I'd show them what singing means! And I did!

WARRINGTON :

You certainly did! Ha! ha! You should have seen Julia's face when you boxed my ears. If the earth had opened her mouth and swallowed you up like Korah, Dathan and the other fellow, it couldn't have opened wider than Julia's.

ETHEL :

Well, she can scowl if she likes. She can't hurt me now.

WARRINGTON :

I'm not so sure of that.

ETHEL :

She'll have to hurry up. We go to-morrow.

WARRINGTON :

Ah, I didn't know. Well, there's nothing like exploding a bomb before you leave, eh? Only it's not always safe—for the operator

GEOFFREY
(*re-entering with* MRS. CASSILIS) :

The carriage is round, Warrington. Lady Rem enham's waiting.

WARRINGTON :

The deuce she is. (*swallows whisky and soda*) I must fly. Good-bye again. Good-bye, Mrs. Cassilis. A thousand thanks for a most interesting evening.

(WARRINGTON *goes out with* GEOFFREY. *Pause.* ETHEL *stands sullen by fireplace.*)

MRS. BORRIDGE
(*yawning cavernously*) :

Well, I think I shall turn in. Good night, Mrs. Cassilis. (*general handshakes*) Coming, Eth?

ETHEL :

In a moment, mother.

(MRS. BORRIDGE *waddles out, with a parting smile from* LADY MARCHMONT. GEOFFREY *returns from seeing* WARRINGTON *off the premises.* MRS. BORRIDGE *wrings his hand affectionately in passing.*)

LADY MARCHMONT :

I must be off, too. And so must you, Mabel. You look tired out. (*kisses* MRS. CASSILIS. GEOFFREY *opens door for them*)

MABEL :

I am a little tired. Good night. (*exeunt* LADY MARCHMONT *and* MABEL)

GEOFFREY :

Are you going, mother?

MRS. CASSILIS :

Not at once. I've a couple of notes to write. (GEOFFREY *crosses to fire.* MRS. CASSILIS *goes to writing table centre, sits facing audience, and appears to begin to write notes. GEOFFREY goes up to ETHEL thoughtfully. A silence. Then he speaks in a low tone.)*

GEOFFREY :

Ethel.

ETHEL :

Yes. *(without looking up)*

GEOFFREY :

Why did you sing that song to-night?

ETHEL
(with a sneer) :

To please Lady Remenham!

GEOFFREY :

But, Ethel! That's not the sort of song Lady Remenham likes at all.

ETHEL
(impatiently) :

To shock her, then.

GEOFFREY :

Ethel!

ETHEL :

I think I managed it, too!

GEOFFREY :

I don't understand. You're joking, aren't you?

ETHEL :

Joking!

GEOFFREY :

I mean, you didn't really do it on purpose, to make
Lady Remenham angry.   I'm sure you didn't.

ETHEL
(*very distinctly*) :

I tell you I did it on purpose, deliberately, to shock
Lady Remenham.   I suppose I ought to know.

GEOFFREY
(*astonished*) :

But why?   What made you do such a thing?

ETHEL
(*savagely*) :

I did it because I chose.   Is that plain enough?

GEOFFREY :

Still, you must have had a reason.   (*no answer,*
suspiciously)   Did that fellow Warrington tell you
to sing it?

ETHEL
(*snaps*) :

No.

GEOFFREY :

I thought perhaps. . . . Anyhow, promise
me not to sing such a song again here.   (*silence*)
You will promise?

ETHEL :

Pooh !

GEOFFREY :

Ethel, be reasonable.   You must know you can't
go on doing that sort of thing here.   When we are

married we shall live down here. You must con-
form to the ideas of the people round you. They
may seem to you narrow and ridiculous, but you
can't alter them.

ETHEL:

You don't think them narrow and ridiculous, I
suppose?

GEOFFREY:

No. In this case I think they are right. In
many cases.

ETHEL:

Sorry I can't agree with you.

GEOFFREY
(*gently*) :

Ethel, dear, don't let's quarrel about a silly thing
like this. If you are going to marry me you *must*
take my judgment on a matter of this kind.

ETHEL
(*defiantly*) :

Must I?

GEOFFREY:

Yes.

ETHEL:

Then I won't. So there. I shall do just exactly
as I please. And if you don't like it you can do the
other thing. I'm not going to be bullied by you.

GEOFFREY
(*reasoning with her*) :

My dear Ethel, I'm sure I am never likely to bully
you, or to do or say anything that is unkind. But
on a point like this I can't give way.

ETHEL :

Very well, Geoff.   If you think that you'd better break off our engagement, that's all.

GEOFFREY :

Ethel!   (*with horror*)

ETHEL
(*impatiently*) :

Well, there's nothing to make faces about, is there?

GEOFFREY :

You don't *mean* that.   You don't mean you *want* our engagement to come to an end.

ETHEL :

Never mind what *I* want.   What do *you* want?

GEOFFREY
(*astonished*) :

Of course I want it to go on.   You know that.

ETHEL
(*gesture of despair*) :

Very well, then.   You'd better behave accordingly.   And now, if you've finished your lecture, I'll go to bed.   Good night. (*goes out, with a nod to* MRS. CASSILIS, *who kisses her good night gently.* GEOFFREY *holds door open for her to go out, then goes and stands by fire.* MRS. CASSILIS, *who has watched this scene while appearing to be absorbed in her notes, now rises to go to her room*)

MRS. CASSILIS
(*cheerfully*):

Well, I must be off, too! Good night, Geoffrey.
(*kisses him*)

GEOFFREY
(*absently*):

Good night, mother. (MRS. CASSILIS *goes slowly
towards door*) Mother.

MRS. CASSILIS
(*turning*):

Yes, Geoff.

GEOFFREY:

Mother, you don't think I was unreasonable in
what I said to Ethel, do you?

MRS. CASSILIS
(*seems to think it over*):

No, Geoff.

GEOFFREY:

Or unkind?

MRS. CASSILIS:

No, Geoff.

GEOFFREY:

I was afraid. She took it so strangely.

MRS. CASSILIS:

She's rather over-excited to-night, I think. And
tired, no doubt. (*encouragingly*) She'll be all
right in the morning.

GEOFFREY :

You think I did right to speak to her about that song?

MRS. CASSILIS :

Quite right, dear. Dear Ethel still has a little to learn, and, of course, it will take time. But we must be patient. Meantime, whenever she makes any little mistake, such as she made to-night, I think you should certainly speak to her about it. It will be such a help to her! I don't mean *scold* her, of course, but speak to her gently and kindly, just as you did to-night.

GEOFFREY
(despondently) :

It didn't seem to do any good.

MRS. CASSILIS :

One never knows, dear. Good night. (*kisses him and goes out. He stands thoughtfully looking into the fire, and the curtain falls*)

ACT IV.

SCENE :—*The morning-room at Deynham. Time, after breakfast next day. A pleasant room, with French windows at the back open on to terrace. The sun is shining brilliantly. There is a door to hall on the left. On the opposite side of the room is the fireplace. When the curtain rises* MABEL *and* GEOFFREY *are on the stage.* GEOFFREY *stands by the fireplace.* MABEL *is standing by the open window. He looks rather out of sorts and dull.*

MABEL :

What a lovely day.

GEOFFREY
(*absently*) :

Not bad. (*pulls out cigarette case*)

MABEL :

I'm sure you smoke too much, Geoffrey.

GEOFFREY
(*smiles*) :

I think not. (*enter* MRS. CASSILIS *from hall*)

MRS. CASSILIS :

Not gone out yet, dears? Why, Mabel, you've not got your habit on.

MABEL :

We're not going to ride this morning.

MRS. CASSILIS
(*surprised*) :

Not going to ride?

MABEL :

No. We've decided to stay at home to-day for a change.

MRS. CASSILIS :

But why, dear?

MABEL
(*hesitating*) :

I don't know. We just thought so. That's all.

MRS. CASSILIS :

But you must have some reason.   You and Geoffrey haven't been quarrelling, have you?

MABEL
(*laughing*) :

Of course not.

MRS. CASSILIS :

Then why aren't you going to ride?

MABEL :

Well, we thought Ethel might be dull if we left
her all alone.

MRS. CASSILIS :

Nonsense, dears.   *I'll* look after Ethel.   Go up
and change, both of you, at once.   Ethel would be
dreadfully grieved if you gave up your ride for her.
Ethel's not selfish.   She would never allow you or
Geoffrey to give up a pleasure on her account.
(*crosses to bell*)

GEOFFREY :

Well, Mabel, what do you say?   (*going to window*)   It is a ripping day.

MABEL :

If Mrs. Cassilis thinks so.

MRS. CASSILIS :

Of course I think so.   Run away, dears, and get
your things on.   I'll tell them to send round the
horses.   (*rings*)

GEOFFREY :

'All right.   Just for an hour.   Come on, Mabel.

I'll race you to the end of the passage. (they *run
out* together, *nearly upsetting footman who enters
at the same moment*)

MRS. CASSILIS :

Lady Mabel and Mr. Geoffrey are going out riding. Tell them to send the horses round. And
tell Hallard I want to see him about those roses.
I'm going into the garden now.

· FOOTMAN :

Very well, madam. (exit FOOTMAN)
(MRS. CASSILIS *goes out* into *the garden. A moment
later* MRS. BORRIDGE *and* ETHEL *come in from the
hall.*)

MRS. BORRIDGE `

(*looking round,* then *going to easy-chair*) :
Mrs. Cassilis isn't here?

ETHEL
(*sulky*) :

I dare say she's with the housekeeper.

MRS. BORRIDGE :

Very likely. (*picks up newspap*er) Give me a
cushion, there's a good girl. (ETHEL *does so*) Lady
Marchmont isn't down yet, I suppose.

ETHEL :

No. (*turns away*)

MRS. BORRIDGE
(*putting* down *paper*) :

What's the matter, dearie? You look awfully
down.

ETHEL:

Nothing. (*goes to window and stares out into the sunlight*)

MRS. BORRIDGE:

I wish Lady Marchmont came down to breakfast of a morning.

ETHEL
(*shrugs*):

Do you?

MRS. BORRIDGE:

Yes. It's dull without her. She and I are getting quite chummy.

ETHEL
(*irritably, swinging round*):

Chummy! My dear mother, Lady Marchmont's only laughing at you.

MRS. BORRIDGE:

Nonsense, Ethel. Laughing at *me*, indeed! I should like to see her!

ETHEL:

That's just it, mother. You never will.

MRS. BORRIDGE:

Pray, what do you mean by *that*, miss?

ETHEL
(*hopeless*):

Oh, it doesn't matter. (*goes to fireplace and leans arm on mantelpiece, depressed*)

MRS. BORRIDGE:

Now you're sneering at me, and I won't 'ave it— have it. (*silence*) Do you 'ear?

ETHEL:

Yes, I *hear.* (*stares down at fender*)

MRS. BORRIDGE:

Very well, then. Don't let me 'ave any more of it. (*grumbling to herself*) Laughing, indeed! (*pause. Recovering her composure*) Where's Geoffy?

ETHEL:

I don't know.

MRS. BORRIDGE:

Out riding, I suppose?

ETHEL:

Very likely.

MRS. BORRIDGE:

'E only finished breakfast just before **us.**

ETHEL:

He, mother.

MRS. BORRIDGE:

Dear, dear, 'ow you do go on! You leave my aitches alone. *They're* all right.

ETHEL
(*sighs*):

I wish they were! (*pause*) You've not forgotten we're going away to-day, mother?

MRS. BORRIDGE:

To-day? 'Oo says so?

ETHEL:

We were only invited for a week.

MRS. BORRIDGE:

Were we, dearie? I don't remember.

ETHEL:

I do.   There's a train at 12.15, if you'll ask Mrs.
Cassilis about the carriage.

MRS. BORRIDGE
(*flustered*):

But I've not let Jane know.   She won't be expecting us.

ETHEL:

We can telegraph.

MRS. BORRIDGE:

Can't we stay another day or two?   I'm sure Mrs.
Cassilis won't mind.   And I'm very comfortable
here.

ETHEL
(*firmly*):

No, mother.

MRS. BORRIDGE:

Why not?

ETHEL
(*exasperated*):

In the first place because we haven't been asked.
In the second, because I don't want to.

MRS. BORRIDGE:

Don't want to?

ETHEL
(*snappishly*):

No.   I'm sick and tired of this place.

MRS. BORRIDGE:

Are you, dearie?   *I* thought we were gettin' on
first rate.

ETHEL :

Did you? Anyhow, we're going, thank goodness, and that's enough. Don't forget to speak to Mrs. Cassilis. I'll go upstairs and pack. (*as she is crossing the room to go out* MRS. CASSILIS *enters from garden and meets her. She stops.* MRS. CASSILIS *kisses her affectionately*)

MRS. CASSILIS :

Going out, Ethel dear? Good morning. (*greets* MRS. BORRIDGE)

ETHEL :

Good morning.

MRS. CASSILIS
(*putting her arm in* ETHEL'S *and leading her up to window*) :

Isn't it a lovely day? I woke at five. I believe it was the birds singing under my window.

ETHEL :

Did you, Mrs. Cassilis? (*enter* LADY MARCHMONT)

LADY MARCHMONT :

Good morning, Adelaide. (*kisses her*) Late again, I'm afraid. (*shakes hands with* ETHEL)

MRS. CASSILIS
(*sweetly*) :
Another of your headaches, dear? I'm so sorry.

LADY MARCHMONT
(*ignoring the rebuke*) :
Good morning, Mrs. Borridge. I hope *you* slept well.

MRS. BORRIDGE :

Sound as a bell.   But, then, I was always a one-
ner to sleep.   My old man, when 'e was alive, used
to say 'e never knew anyone sleep like me.   And
snore !   Why 'e declared it kep' 'im awake 'alf the
night.   But *I* never noticed it.

LADY MARCHMONT
(*sweetly*) :

That must have been a great consolation for Mr.
Borridge.

MRS. BORRIDGE :

Your 'usband snore?

LADY MARCHMONT :
(*laughing*) :

No.

MRS. BORRIDGE :

Thinks it's low per'aps . . .   They used to
say snorin' comes from sleepin' with your mouth
open, but *I* don't know.   What do *you* think?

LADY MARCHMONT :

I really don't know, dear Mrs. Borridge.   I must
think it over.   (LADY MARCHMONT *takes chair by*
MRS. BORRIDGE.   *They converse in dumb show.*
ETHEL *and* MRS. CASSILIS *come down stage*)

MRS. CASSILIS :

What a pretty blouse you've got on to-day, dear.

ETHEL :

Is it, Mrs. Cassilis?

MRS. CASSILIS :

Sweetly pretty.   It goes so well with your eyes.
You've lovely eyes, you know.

ETHEL:

Do you think so?

MRS. CASSILIS:

Of course. So does Geoff.

ETHEL
(*disengaging herself*):

Oh, Geoff—— Well, I must go upstairs. (*to*
MRS. BORRIDGE *in passing*) Don't forget, mummy.
(*exit* ETHEL)

MRS. BORRIDGE:

What, dearie? Oh, yes. Ethel says we must
be packin' our traps, Mrs. Cassilis.

MRS. CASSILIS
(*startled*):

Packing?

MRS. BORRIDGE:

Yes. She says we mustn't outstay our welcome.
She's proud, is my girlie.

MRS. CASSILIS
(*with extreme cordiality*):

But you're not thinking of leaving us? Oh, you
mustn't do that. Geoff would be so disappointed.
And so should I.

MRS. BORRIDGE:

I don't want to go, I'm sure. Only Ethel said—

MRS. CASSILIS:

There must be some mistake. I counted on you
for quite a long visit.

MRS. BORRIDGE:

Ethel said we were only asked for week.

MRS. CASSILIS:

But that was before I really knew you, wasn't it.
It's quite different now.

MRS. BORRIDGE
(*purring* deli*ght*edly):

If you feel that, Mrs. Cassilis—

MRS. CASSILIS :

Of course I feel it.   I hope you'll stay quite a
lon*g* time yet.

MRS. BORRIDGE

(com*p*lacent, *appealing* to LADY MARCHMONT, *who*
nod*s* **sympathy**):

There !   I told Ethel how it was.

MRS. CASSILIS
(*anxious*):

Ethel doesn't *want* to go, does she?

MRS. BORRIDGE:

Oh, *no*.   She'd be delighted to stop on.   Only
she thought——

MRS. CASSILIS

(*determined to leave* MRS. BORRIDGE *no opportunity
to hedge*):

Very well, then.   That's settled.   You'll stay
with us till Geoff and I go to Scotland.   That won't
be till the   end   of August.   You promise?

MRS. BORRIDGE:

Thank you, Mrs. Cassilis.   I call that real hospitable !   (*rising*)   And now I'll run upstairs and

tell **my** girl, or she'll be packing my black satin before I've time to stop her. She's so 'asty. And I always say nothing spoils things like packing, especially satins. They do crush so. (MRS. BORRIDGE *waddles out. As soon as the* door *closes* MRS. CASSILIS *heaves a deep sigh of relief, showing how alarmed she had been lest the* BORRIDGES *should really take their departure. For a moment there is silence. Then* LADY MARCHMONT, *who has watched this scene with full appreciation of its ironic humour, speaks*)

LADY MARCHMONT:

How you fool that old woman!

MRS. CASSILIS:

So do *you*, dear.

LADY MARCHMONT:

Yes. You'll make me as great a hypocrite as yourself before you've done. When you first began I was shocked at you. But now I feel a dreadful spirit of emulation stealing over me.

MRS. CASSILIS
(*grimly*):

There's always a satisfaction in doing a thing well, isn't there?

LADY MARCHMONT:

You must feel it, then.

MRS. CASSILIS:

Thanks.

LADY MARCHMONT
(*puzzled*):

Do you really want these dreadful people to stay all that time?

MRS. CASSILIS:

Certainly.   And to come back, if necessary, in October.

LADY MARCHMONT:

Good heavens! Why?

MRS. CASSILIS
(sitting):

My dear Margaret, as long as that woman and her daughter are here we *may* get Geoffrey out of their clutches. I thought we should manage it last night.   Last night was a terrible disillusionment for him, poor boy. But I was wrong. It was too soon.

LADY MARCHMONT:

By the way, what did that amusing wretch Major Warrington advise?

MRS. CASSILIS:

I didn't consult him.   I'd no opportunity.   Besides, I couldn't have trusted him.   He might have gone over to the enemy.

LADY MARCHMONT:

Yes.   He was evidently attracted to the girl.

MRS. CASSILIS:

I suppose so.   Major Warrington isn't fastidious where women are concerned.

LADY MARCHMONT:

Still, he knew, of course.

MRS. CASSILIS:

Only what Lady Remenham would have told him. However, his visit wasn't altogether wasted, I think.

LADY MARCHMONT :

That song, you mean.

MRS. CASSILIS :

Yes. He gave poor Ethel a glimpse of the Para-
dise she is turning her back on for ever. London,
music-hall songs, racketty bachelors. And that
made her reckless. The contrast between Major
Warrington, and, say, our dear Rector, can hardly
fail to have gone home to her.

(*Further conversation is interrupted by the entrance
of* ETHEL, *in the worst of tempers.* MRS. CASSILIS
is on her guard at once.)

ETHEL

(*bursting out*) :

Mrs. Cassilis——

MRS. CASSILIS

(*very sweetly, rising and going to her*) :

Ethel, dear, what *is* this I hear? You're not
going to run away from us?

ETHEL

(*doggedly*) :

Indeed, we must, Mrs. Cassilis. You've had us
for a week. We really mustn't stay any longer.

MRS. CASSILIS :

But, my dear, it's deli*ghtful* to have you.

MRS. BORRIDGE

(*who has followed hard after her daughter and now
enters, flushed and rather breathless*) :

There, you see, dearie! What did I tell you?

MRS. CASSILIS :

Geoff would be *terribly* distressed if you went

away. He'd think I hadn't made you comfortable. He'd scold me dreadfully.

ETHEL:

I don't think Geoff will care. (MRS. BORRIDGE *appeals mutely for sympathy to* LADY MARCHMONT, *who hastens to give it in full measure*)

MRS. CASSILIS
(*great solicitude*):

My dear, you've not had any little difference with Geoff? Any quarrel?

ETHEL:

No.

MRS. CASSILIS:

I was so afraid——

ETHEL:

Still, we oughtn't to plant ourselves on you in this way.

MRS. BORRIDGE:

Plant ourselves! Really, dearie, how can you say such things? Plant ourselves!

ETHEL:

Oh, do be quiet, mother. (*stamps her foot*)

MRS. CASSILIS
(*soothing her*):

Anyhow, you can't possibly go to-day. The carriage has gone to Branscombe, and the other horse has cast a shoe. And to-morrow there's a dinner party at Milverton. You'll stay for *that*?

ETHEL:

You're very kind, Mrs. Cassilis, but——

MRS. CASSILIS

(leaving her no time to withdraw):
That's right, my dear.   You'll stay.   And next
week we'll have some young people over to meet
you, and you shall dance all the evening.

MRS. BORRIDGE:

There, Ethel!

ETHEL

(hopeless):
Very well.   If you really wish it.

MRS. CASSILIS:

Of course I wish it.   I'm *so* glad.   I shan't be
able to part with you for a long time yet.   *(kisses
her tenderly.   But* ETHEL *seems too depressed to
answer to these blandishments)*

LADY MARCHMONT
(under her breath):
Really, Adelaide!

MRS. CASSILIS
(sweetly):
Into the garden, did you say, Margaret?   *(taking
her up towards window)*   Very well.   The sun *is*
tempting, isn't it?
*(*MRS. CASSILIS *and her sister sail out.* ETHEL *and
her mother remain, the former in a condition of
frantic exasperation.)*

ETHEL:

Well, mother, you've done it!

MRS. BORRIDGE
(snapping.   She feels she is being goaded unduly):
Done what, dearie?

ETHEL
(*impatiently*):

Oh, you know.

MRS. BORRIDGE:

Do you mean about staying on here? But what could I do? Mrs. Cassilis wouldn't *let* us go. You saw that yourself.

ETHEL:

You might have stood out.

MRS. BORRIDGE:

I did, dearie. I stood out as long as ever I could. But she wouldn't hear of our goin'. You saw that yourself.

ETHEL:

Well, mother, don't say I didn't warn you, that's all.

MRS. BORRIDGE:

Warn me, dearie?

ETHEL
(*breaking out*):

That I was tired of this place. Sick and tired of it! That it was time we were moving.

MRS. BORRIDGE
(*placidly*):

Is that all? I'll remember. (*pause*) How far did you get with the packing?

ETHEL
(*impatiently*):

I don't know.

MRS. BORRIDGE :

You hadn't packed my black satin?

ETHEL :

I don't know. Yes, I think so. I'm not sure.
Don't worry, mother.

MRS. BORRIDGE
(*lamentably*) :

It'll be simply covered with creases. I know it
will. Run up at once, there's a good girl, and shake
it out.

ETHEL
(*snaps*) :

Oh, bother.

MRS. BORRIDGE :

Then I must. How tiresome girls are! Always
in the tantrums!

(*Poor old* MRS. BORRIDGE *ambles out grumbling.*
ETHEL, *left alone, sits scowling furiously at the
carpet and biting her nails. There is a considerable
pause, during which her rage and weariness are
silently expressed. Then* GEOFFREY *and* MABEL
*enter, quite cheerful, in riding things. They make
a curious contrast to the almost tragic figure of
sulkiness which meets their eyes.*)

GEOFFREY
(*cheerfully*) :

Hullo, Ethel! There you are, are you?

ETHEL
(*sulky*) :

You can see me, I suppose.

MABEL :

We didn't get our ride after all.

ETHEL :

Didn't you?   (*turns away*)

MABEL :

No.   Basil has strained one of his sinews, poor darling.   He'll have to lie up for a day or two.

GEOFFREY :

Isn't it hard luck?   It would have been such a glorious day for a ride.   We were going round by Long Winton and up to Tenterden's farm and——

ETHEL
(*snaps*) :

You needn't trouble to tell me.   I don't want to hear.   (*there is an awkward pause after this explosion*)

MABEL :

I think I'll go up and change my habit, Geoff. (GEOFFREY *nods, and* MABEL *goes out.* GEOFFREY *after a moment goes up to* ETHEL, *and lays a hand gently on her shoulder.*)

GEOFFREY :

What is it, Ethel?   Is anything the matter?

ETHEL
(*shaking him off fiercely*) :

Please don't touch me.

GEOFFREY :

Something has happened.   What is it?

ETHEL

(*savagely*) :

Nothing's happened. Nothing ever does happen **here**.

(GEOFFREY *tries to take her hand. She pulls it pettishly away. He slightly shrugs his shoulders. A* long *pause. He rises slowly and turns towards door.*)

ETHEL

(*stopping him*) :

Geoff !

GEOFFREY :

Yes. (*does not turn his head*)

ETHEL :

I want to break off our engagement.

GEOFFREY

(*swinging round, astonished, and not for a moment taking her seriously*) :

My dear girl !

ETHEL :

I think it would be better. Better for both of us.

GEOFFREY

(*still rallying her*) :

Might one ask why ?

ETHEL :

For many reasons. Oh, don't let us go into all that. Just say you release me and there's an end.

GEOFFREY

(*more serious*) :

My dear Ethel. What *is* the matter ? Aren't you *well ?*

ETHEL
(*impatiently*) :

I'm perfectly well.

GEOFFREY :

I don't think you are.   You look quite flushed.   I wish you'd take more exercise.   You'd be ever so much better.

ETHEL
(*goaded to frenzy by this well-meant suggestion,*
GEOFFREY'S *panacea for all human ills*) :

Geoffrey, you're simply maddening.   Do please understand that I know when I'm well and when I'm ill.   There's nothing whatever the matter with me.   I believe you think everything in life would go right if only everyone took a cold bath every morning and spend the rest of the day shooting part-ridges.

GEOFFREY
(quite *simply*) :

Well, there's a lot in that, isn't there?

ETHEL :

Rubbish !

GEOFFREY
(*struck by a brilliant idea*) :

It's not that silly business about the riding again, is it?

ETHEL
(*almost hysterical with exasperation*) :

Oh, no! no!   *Please* believe that I'm not a child, and that I know what I'm saying.   *I want to break off our engagement.*   I don't think we're suited to each other.

GEOFFREY
(*piqued*) :
This is rather sudden, isn't it?

ETHEL
(*sharply*) :
How do you know it's sudden?

GEOFFREY :
But isn't it?

ETHEL :
No. It's not.

GEOFFREY
(*struck* by *a thought*) :
Ethel, has my mother——?

ETHEL :
Your mother has nothing whatever to do with it.

GEOFFREY :
She hasn't said anything?

ETHEL :
Your mother has been everything that's kind and good. In fact, if it hadn't been for her I think I should have broken it off before. But I didn't want to hurt her. (GEOFFREY *rises, and paces the room up and* down *for a moment in thought. Then he turns to her again*)

GEOFFREY :
Ethel, you mustn't come to a decision like this hastily. You must take time to consider.

ETHEL :
Thank you. My mind is quite made up.

GEOFFREY :

Still, you might think it over for a day or two—a week, perhaps. It (*hesitates*) . . . . it wouldn't be fair of me to take you at your word in this way.

ETHEL :

Why not?

GEOFFREY
(*hesitates*) :

You might—regret it afterwards.

ETHEL
(*with a short laugh*) :

You're very modest.

GEOFFREY
(*nettled*) :

Oh, I'm not vain enough to imagine that you would find anything to regret in *me*. *I'm* a commonplace fellow enough.   But there are other things which a girl has to consider in marriage, aren't there?   Position.   Money.   If you broke off our engagement now, mightn't you regret these later on (*slight touch of bitterness*) however little you regret *me?*

ETHEL
(*touched*) :

Geoff, dear, I'm sorry I hurt you.   I didn't mean to.   You're a good fellow.   Far too good for me. And I know you mean it kindly when you ask me to take time, and all that.   But my mind's quite made up.   Don't let's say any more about it.

GEOFFREY
(*slowly, and a little sadly*):

You don't love me any more, then?

ETHEL :

No. (*decisively*) I don't love you any more. Perhaps I never did love you really, Geoff. I don't know.

GEOFFREY :

I loved *you*, Ethel.

ETHEL :

I wonder.

GEOFFREY :

You know I did.

ETHEL :

You thought you did. But that's not always the same thing, is it? Many a girl takes a man's fancy for a moment. Yet people say one only loves once, don't they? (*pause*)

GEOFFREY

(*hesitating again*) :

Ethel . . . I don't know how to say it. . . . You'll laugh at me again. . . . But . . . you're sure you're not doing this on *my* account?

ETHEL :

On *your* account?

GEOFFREY :

Yes. To spare me. Because you think I ought to marry in my own class, as Lady Remenham would say?

ETHEL :

No.

GEOFFREY ?

Quite sure?

ETHEL
(nods):

Quite.   (turns away)

GEOFFREY
(frankly puzzled):

Then I can't understand it!

ETHEL
(turning on him impatiently):

My dear Geoff, is it impossible for you to understand that I don't want to marry you?   That if I
married you I should be bored to death?   That I
loathe the life down here among your highly respectable friends? That if I had to live here with
you I should yawn myself into my grave in six
months?

GEOFFREY
(astonished):

Don't you like Deynham?

ETHEL:

No. I detest it. Oh, it's pretty enough, I suppose, and the fields are very green, and the view
from Milverton Hill is much admired.   And you
live all alone in a great park, and you've horses and
dogs, and a butler and two footmen. But that's not
enough for me. I want life, people, lots of people.
If I lived down here I should go blue-mouldy in
three weeks.   I'm town-bred, a true cockney.   I
want streets and shops and gas lamps.   I don't
want your carriages and pair.   Give me a penny
omnibus.

GEOFFREY :

Ethel)

ETHEL :

Now you're shocked. It *is* vulgar, isn't it? But
I'm vulgar. And I'm not ashamed of it. Now
you know. (*another pause.* GEOFFREY, *in pained
surprise, ponders* deeply. *At last he speaks*)

GEOFFREY :

It's all over, then?

ETHEL
(*nodding flippantly*) :

All over and done with. I surrender my claim to
everything, the half of your worldly goods, of your
mother's worldly goods, of your house, your park,
your men-servants and maid-servants, your aristo-
cratic relations. Don't let's forget your aristocra-
tic relations. I surrender them all. There's my
hand on it. (*stretches* it *out*)

GEOFFREY
(*pained*) :

Don't, Ethel.

ETHEL
(*with genuine surprise*) :

My dear Geoff, you don't mean to say you're
sorry! You ought to be flinging your cap in the air
at regaining your liberty. Why, I believe there are
tears in your eyes! Actually tears! Let me look.
(*turns his face to her*)

GEOFFREY
(*pulling it away sulkily*) :

You don't suppose a fellow likes being thrown
over like this, do you?

ETHEL :

Vanity, my dear Geoff! Mere vanity.

GEOFFREY
(hotly) :

It's not *!*

ETHEL
(suddenly serious) :

Geoff, do you *want* our engagement to go on?
Do you *want* to marry me still? *(he turns to her
impulsively)* Do you *love* me still? *(checks him)*
No, Geoff.   Think before you speak.   On your
honour!   (GEOFFREY *is silent.*)   There, you see!
Come, dear, cheer up.   It's best as it is.   Give me
a kiss.   The last one. *(she goes to* GEOFFREY *and
holds up her face to be kissed.   He kisses her on
the forehead)* And now I'll run upstairs and tell
mother. *(laughs)* Poor mother!   Won't she make
a shine!

*(*ETHEL *goes out recklessly.* GEOFFREY, *left alone,
looks round the room in a dazed way.   Takes out
cigarette case automatically, goes to writing table
for match.   Just as he is lighting cigarette* MRS.
CASSILIS *enters from garden, followed a moment
later by* LADY MARCHMONT. *He throws cigarette
away unlighted.)*

MRS. CASSILIS :

'All alone, Geoffrey?

GEOFFREY :

Yes, mother.

MRS. CASSILIS :

Where's Ethel?

GEOFFREY :

Mother—Ethel's . . . *(sees* LADY MARCH-
MONT.   *Pause)* Good morning, Aunt Margaret.

LADY MARCHMONT:

Good morning.

MRS. CASSILIS:

Well, dear?

GEOFFREY:

Mother (*plunging into his subject*) a terrible thing has happened. Ethel was here a moment ago, and she has broken off our engagement.

LADY MARCHMONT:

Broken it off!

MRS. CASSILIS
(*immensely sympathetic*):

Broken it off, dear? Surely not?

GEOFFREY:

Yes.

MRS. CASSILIS:

Oh, *poor* Geoffrey. (*going to him*) Did she say why?

GEOFFREY
(*dully*):

Only that it had all been a mistake. She was tired of it all, and didn't like the country, and— that's all, I think.

MRS. CASSILIS
(*anxious*):

My poor boy. And I thought her so happy with us. (*laying hand caressingly on his shoulder as he sits with head bowed*) You don't think we've been to blame—*I've* been to blame—in any way, do you? Perhaps we ought **to** have amused her more?

GEOFFREY:

Not you, mother. You've always been sweet and good to her. Always. She said so.

MRS. CASSILIS:

I'm glad of that, dear.
(Enter MRS. BORRIDGE, *furiously angry, followed by* ETHEL, *vainly trying to detain or silence her.* GEOFFREY *retreats up stage, where* MRS. BORRIDGE *for a moment does not notice him.*)

MRS. BORRIDGE
(*raging*):

Where's, Geoff? Leave me alone, Ethel. Where's Geoff?

ETHEL:

He's not here, mother. And Mrs. Cassilis is. Do be quiet.

GEOFFREY
(*coming between them*):

I'm here. What is it, Mrs. Borridge?

MRS. BORRIDGE:

Oh, Geoffy, what *is* this Ethel's been telling me? You haven't reely broke off your engagement, have you?

ETHEL:

Nonsense, mother. *I* broke it off, as I told you.

MRS. BORRIDGE:

But you didn't mean it, dearie. It's all a mistake. Just a little tiff.

ETHEL
(*firmly*):

No!

MRS. BORRIDGE
(obstinately):

Yes, it is. It'll blow over. You wouldn't be so
unkind to poor Geoffy.

ETHEL:

Mother, don't be a fool. It doesn't take anybody in. Come upstairs and let's get on with our
packing.

MRS. BORRIDGE
(stamps foot):

Be quiet, Ethel, when I tell you. Lady Marchmont, won't *you* speak to her? Undutiful girl. I
should like to *whip* her! (ETHEL *turns away in
despair*)

LADY MARCHMONT
(soothingly):

Ah, well, dear Mrs. Borridge, perhaps young
people know best about these things.

MRS. BORRIDGE
(excited *and angry*):

Know best! know best! How should they know
best? They don't know *anything*. They're as
ignorant as they are uppish. (*growing tearful*) And
to think 'ow I've worked for that girl! 'Ow I've
slaved for 'er, denied myself for 'er. (*breaking
down*) I did so want 'er to be respectable. I
'aven't always been respectable myself, and I know
the value of it. (*subsides into chair, almost hysterical, and no longer realising what she is saying*)

ETHEL:

Oh, hush, mother!

MRS. BORRIDGE
(angry again):

I won't 'ush, so there! I'm your mother, and
I won't be trod on. *I* find someone to marry you—
a better match than ever you'll find for yourself,
miss—and this is 'ow I'm treated! (begins to cry)

ETHEL
(taking her arm):

Mother, mother, do come away.

MRS. BORRIDGE
(breaking down altogether):

And now to 'ave to begin all over again. And
young men ain't so green as they used to be. Not
by a long way. They're cunning most of them.
They take a deal of catchin'. And I'm gettin' an
old woman. Oh, she might 'ave spared me this.

MRS. CASSILIS
(almost sorry for her):

Mrs. Borridge—Mrs. Borridge.

MRS. BORRIDGE
(refusing to be comforted):

But she's no natural affection. That's what it
is. She doesn't love 'er mother. She's 'eadstrong
and wilful, and never paid the least attention to
what I told 'er. (burst of tears) But I do think she
might 'ave let 'im break it off. Then there'd 'ave
been a breach of promise, and that's always something. That's what I always say to girls: "Leave
them to break it off, dearies. And then there'll be
a breach of promise, *and* damages." That's if
you've got something on paper. But (fresh burst

of tears) she never *would* get anything on paper. She never paid the least regard to her old mother. She's an undutiful girl, and that's 'ow it is. (*goes off* into incoherent *sobs*)

BUTLER :

Lady Remenham.

MRS. CASSILIS
(*rising hastily*) :

The drawing-room, Watson. (*she is, however, too late to stop* WATSON *from showing in* LADY REMENHAM)

LADY REMENHAM
(*sailing in, with breezy cheerfulness*) :

How do you do, Adelaide? How do you do, Margaret? I've just driven Algernon to the station, and I thought I'd leave this for you as I passed. (*gives book*)

MRS. BORRIDGE :

She's an undutiful daughter. That's what she is. (*snorting and sobbing*)

LADY REMENHAM
(*perceiving for the first time that something unusual is going on*) :

Eh?

MRS. CASSILIS :

Mrs. Borridge is not quite herself just now. Dear Ethel has decided that she does not wish to continue her engagement to my son, and Mrs. Borridge has only just heard the news.

LADY REMENHAM :
(*scarcely able to believe her ears*) :

Not wish——!

Mrs. Cassilis
(hastily, checking her):

No.   This has naturally upset us all very much.
It was so very sudden.

Lady Remenham :

Well, I must say—— (luckily she does not do so,
but takes refuge in silence)

Mrs. Borridge
(burst of grief):

Oh, why didn't she get something on paper?
Letters is best.   Men are that slippy!   I always
told her to get something on paper.   (breaks down
completely)

Ethel :

Come away, mother.   (takes her firmly by the
arm)   Will you please order the carriage, Mrs.
Cassilis?   (leads Mrs. Borridge off, sobbing and
gulping to the last)

Lady Remenham
(sitting down, with a triumphant expression on her amiable countenance):

Geoffrey, will you tell the coachman to drive round
to the stables?   I shall stay to luncheon!

(It is impossible adequately to represent the tone in
which Lady Remenham announces this intention.   It
is that of a victorious general occupying the field,
from which he has beaten the enemy with bag and
baggage.   Luckily, Geoffrey is too depressed to
notice anything.   He goes out without a word—
and the curtain falls.)

Lightning Source UK Ltd.
Milton Keynes UK
UKOW06f1923131117
312695UK00006B/872/P